BUYING
QUALITY

ROSS H. JOHNSON
RICHARD T. WEBER

Buying Quality

HOW PURCHASING,
QUALITY CONTROL,
AND SUPPLIERS
WORK TOGETHER

FRANKLIN WATTS 1985   NEW YORK TORONTO

Library of Congress Cataloging in Publication Data

Johnson, Ross H.
Buying quality.

Includes bibliographical references and index.
I. Quality control.   I. Weber, Richard T.   II. Title.
TS156.J66   1985   658.5'62   84-25775
ISBN 0-531-09588-6

This book was developed in part under a grant from
the National Contract Management Association

CONTENTS

CHAPTER TWO
SPECIFICATION OF REQUIREMENTS

CHAPTER THREE
SUPPLIER EVALUATION AND SELECTION

CHAPTER FOUR
WORKING RELATIONSHIPS WITH SUPPLIERS

CHAPTER FIVE
LEGAL ASPECTS

CHAPTER SIX
EVIDENCE OF CONFORMANCE

CHAPTER SEVEN
INSPECTION AND TEST

CHAPTER NINE
STRATEGY AND MOTIVATION
FOR SUPPLIER QUALITY

FIGURES

BUYING
QUALITY

IMPORTANCE OF
QUALITY
IN PROCUREMENT

No one can dispute that the vital interests of any company depend upon the satisfactory performance of products and services rendered by its suppliers. Deficiencies in supplied products or services can increase spoilage, reduce sales, delay delivery schedules, and reduce productivity. These in turn have an adverse effect on profits of the company, and may even jeopardize the company's ability to stay in business. Although these ideas are not new, their importance has become increasingly evident over the past decade as many U.S. companies have lost large shares of their market to foreign competitors. This does not mean that price is of any less importance than it has been in the past, but rather that buyers and consumers are paying greater attention to quality as a comparative factor when selecting products.

The costs of purchased materials, parts, and components make up a substantial portion of the total direct costs for many companies, though the proportion varies considerably from company to company and from one product to another within any company. Often the procured items are complex or perform vital functions in the product; therefore it becomes important for any company to place emphasis on assuring the quality of procured items. It is not always easy to obtain this assurance. Since the manufacturing and quality control operations of the supplier are not under the direct control or observation of the primary manufacturer (contractor), it is necessary to implement tasks and controls that will provide the needed assurance. When a supplier is being considered for an order, the quality of products supplied previously becomes a primary consideration. If quality has been inadequate and the supplier shows little interest in correcting it, a reorder usually goes to a different supplier.

The purchasing department has the primary responsibility for administration of the subcontract with the supplier. Other departments, like engineering and quality control, have the technical know-how about the function of the items and techniques available to assure a good product. The departments, by working together, can establish a program that will assure that a quality product will be received when scheduled and at a competitive cost.

DEFINING QUALITY

A quality product is defined by some people as one that will satisfy the needs of the customer. Others say that a quality product is one that conforms to the standards established for it. While one might say that a Cadillac has greater quality than a Chevrolet, this is a different use of the word *quality*. As used in the quality control profession, the term *quality* applies to either of these automobiles or any other products if they conform to the standards (or requirements) established for them. This holds true as long as these standards result in a product that meets the needs of the user. We might then conclude that quality means fitness for intended use or reasonable use.

An understanding of the meaning of quality is important as it applies to products and purchased materials. Quality consists of many properties of the product. Each of these properties or characteristics must be defined so that quality can be measured and achieved consistently. It is not satisfactory to speak of quality only in terms of good or bad. In the case of purchased items, the definitions of the required quality characteristics must be such that the supplier can know what is wanted, and both the supplier and the using company can measure to determine whether the quality characteristics have been achieved. These needed characteristics should be defined in the purchase order or subcontract so that both parties know and agree to the requirements. There are many characteristics associated with each product. The following are some examples of characteristics that may need to be defined and verified:

1. Physical dimensions
2. Appearance, color, finish, surface roughness
3. Weight, density, porosity, texture, tensile strength
4. Performance (or operation)
5. Life, reliability
6. Shelf life, durability, fracture resistance
7. Limits on product's noise or pollutants; freedom from foreign matter or impurity
8. Utility, efficiency, economy in use
9. Ability to be used with other products
10. Ability to perform in specified environments, under certain stresses, or under other use condition such as the presence of heat, cold, moisture, vibration, shock, or radiation
11. Serviceability or ease of repair and maintenance
12. Documentation on product manufacture and testing

The absence of any of these characteristics, where needed, in the manufacture or testing of a product, results in a product quality deficiency.

PRODUCTS OR SERVICES

Quality pertains to services as well as products. A substantial proportion of businesses are considered to be service industries and many contracts or subcontracts involve services. These services can include advertising, contract engineers, market research, cafeteria services, janitorial services, trucking or delivery services, and repair and maintenance services. As with the purchaser of products, the buyer of services needs to be concerned with price, quality, and schedule considerations. As this book proceeds, we will see that all aspects of a good supplier quality program apply to service subcontracts as well as subcontracts for products. Definition of requirements, source selection, and evaluation of what is furnished are as important in the procurement of services as they are in the procurement of tangible items.

The definition of a service, and of the quality characteristics sought in a service, may be more difficult to establish than for a product. This does not mean, however, that careful definition is less important. If the quality and delivery requirements can be closely defined, then the successful bidder can be selected on a price basis. If, however, the company purchasing a service fails to define the quality expected, then the buyer will not be able to define the full scope of the service, and source selection will be more complex. This makes the buyer's job more difficult since he can rely only on knowledge of prior services performed by a supplier, obtained either through direct experience or through reports from others who have used the services.

As with a product, the evaluation of service quality must consider the level of quality plus the degree of consistency, or freedom from excessive variability. Factors affecting variability of service quality can be absenteeism, disruptions to service, service during unexpected breakdowns or adverse weather conditions, and handling of responsibilities under other adverse or unexpected situations.

In summary, we can conclude that the quality considerations in purchasing services are similar to those in purchasing manufactured items. They include establishment of quality standards, evaluation of quality, and assignment of responsibilities.

The benefits of achieved quality and the costs of nonconformance in procuring services are comparable to those encountered in procuring products.

A COMPANY COMMITMENT

In times past, quality was produced by craftsmen, relying on simple tools and the skill of their hands. A little later, quality often referred to an after-the-fact evaluation by quality control people of goods produced by the manufacturing people. If items failed to conform, they would be returned to manufacturing to be made right, scrapped if repair was impossible, or in some cases shipped to unknowing customers. In today's more competitive environment, however, concepts such as AQL (Acceptable Quality Level) are no longer sufficient in themselves. The management of quality now requires an overall company commitment. Emphasis on quality must be evident in each management action or decision. Each management decision must be reached after careful consideration of its impact on quality. Otherwise, employee attitudes toward quality will reflect management's failure to assign it a higher priority.

The purchasing organization has a heavy responsibility in the pursuit of quality, since supplier items have a significant impact on the overall product quality, and the supplier looks to the buyer for direction. Philip Crosby states it well when he says: "Quality improvement is built on getting everyone to do it right the first time."[1] This concept certainly applies to getting the supplier to do it right the first time. The buyer must place emphasis on quality as well as price and schedule. However, this increased emphasis on quality by purchasing is not always easily achieved. In evaluating bids and products, it is easy to compare price and schedule in selecting a supplier. Evaluating quality is more difficult for a buyer since facts and evidence may not be available. The buyer often depends on the opinion of others as

1. Philip B. Crosby, *Quality Without Tears*, (New York: McGraw-Hill, 1984), 59.

to quality of a supplier's products. Companies that choose not to demand quality from suppliers, however, may end up being out of business.

> *Case Example.* A supplier was providing a system that included, as a small but critical part, a complex electromechanical unit. When received, the electromechanical units exhibited various malfunctions. Although the supplier committed during phone conversations to correct the defects, the problems continued. When a quality engineer visited the supplier's facility he found a good, well-documented quality system, well-trained and knowledgeable inspection personnel, and good product evaluation techniques. However, throughout the visit the quality engineer detected management emphasis on shipping products to meet delivery schedules ahead of meeting quality standards. The quality engineer reported this finding to the manager of purchasing, who worked with the supplier company president to establish the priority of meeting delivery schedules, without any sacrifice of quality.

PART OF STRATEGY

The strategy developed by a firm must deal with external and internal resources. Although many leading companies have always viewed product quality as an important element of their strategy, the late 1970s and early 1980s have witnessed a change in attitude toward quality by many more companies. In the past, their higher management may have tended to view quality as something that should be there. It was viewed as being controlled by inspection rather than as a budget with goals, objectives, and measured results requiring continuous top management attention. Company goals often lacked specific quality objectives to go along with other elements of the company operating plans. The company strategy often did not include achievement of quality. To be competitive, a company's strategy must include both internal quality objectives and quality control standards, as well as objectives for suppliers of materials, products, and services.

When labor was cheap, it was feasible to simply sort bad items from the good and send the bad ones back to be replaced or fixed. If the defect was not recognized and was sent on to the customer who used the product, it could be returned for repair, or serviced at a user location. Skyrocketing maintenance and repair costs—along with consumer safety regulations and costly court decisions related to product liability—have made everyone increasingly concerned with quality. It is costly for manufacturers to handle, service, repair, and return defective supplier parts. A production line shutdown for lack of parts can result in an enormous loss. Management has become more and more concerned with quality as customers demand warranties, federal agencies require recalls, and courts give large awards resulting from defective products. Suppliers who have adjusted to these concepts have become more competitive in a market where price and delivery are not the only measurable factors.

PERCEPTIONS OF A SUPPLIER

A supplier, in dealing with the purchasing agent, responds to those factors perceived to be of greater importance. If the buyer places emphasis upon cost and schedule in negotiating a purchase order, it seems logical that the supplier will perceive these to be of greater importance than other factors such as service and quality. We might conclude that the inclusion of quality requirements in the subcontract is important. Besides, the purchasing agent who is knowledgeable in quality and who stresses quality to the supplier along with price and delivery, will in the long run be rewarded with greater quality efforts on the part of the supplier and perhaps fewer problems on the subcontract.

DECLINE IN QUALITY?

Several U.S. products that were traditionally considered by the world to be superior have of late been perceived as inferior. Examples are automobiles, electronic equipment, and textiles. Are we saying that the quality of U.S. products has declined? Actually, the quality of U.S. products is higher now than it has ever been. Compare the latest television, computer, or typewriter with an older model to establish this fact. What then has happened to foster this perception of diminished quality? Basically, some foreign companies have increased their share of the

FIG. 1–1.
COMPARATIVE QUALITY TRENDS

market by providing superior quality at equal or lower prices. We can conclude that the quality of U.S. products has not declined, but rather that products manufactured in other countries have surged past ours in quality while beating ours in costs. Figure 1-1 illustrates this trend.

SOURCES OF POOR QUALITY

For any company there are three primary sources of inadequate quality: (1) inadequate definition of product or its intended use, (2) defects introduced due to in-house causes, and (3) defects originating in purchased items, materials, or processes. The third category would include defects originating in items supplied by other plants of the same company. The fact that the source is part of the same company does not usually make a difference in our approach to quality achievement. Quality problems often arise because of different goals, different locations, different people, or involvement with different lines of products. In this book when we speak of suppliers, we will assume that our concepts apply to makers of goods produced in any separate facility.

EXCUSES FOR POOR QUALITY

We often hear of the Japanese success in achievement of quality in their products. Perhaps this should be viewed as a setback in the salability of U.S. products in world markets. Then we are told that we should attempt to learn and apply the techniques the Japanese employ. Those making these statements have forgotten (or do not realize) that these techniques were taught to the Japanese by people from this country, such as Drs. Deming and Juran. The message they brought to the Japanese was to emphasize quality. The techniques they used were also available to U.S. firms. In other words, the technical capability for production of good quality made available through the knowledge of our quality experts was accepted and has simply been better utilized by the Japanese over the past decade or more.

We hear further that the culture of the Japanese permits them to better apply these quality concepts. Again we seem to forget that in the 1930s, "Made in Japan" implied that a product was of poor quality, and that there has been little change in Japanese culture in the past seventy years or more. The idea that culture determines a nation's ability to produce quality products, then, is fallacious. A company that must achieve quality in its products cannot afford to accept such delusions and excuses from its own people or from its suppliers as it pursues its quality objectives. There is no technical inability of U.S. firms to compete in the production of quality goods for sale in world markets. Companies that previously held that finance and marketing were the key elements of success strategy are beginning to recognize that product quality can also be a strategic weapon in the competition for worldwide market share.

QUALITY AND PRODUCTIVITY

In the past, managers often thought of quality and productivity as opposites, maintaining that when one was increased, it was at the expense of the other. This fallacy has hindered quality improvement in many companies. More recent experience shows the reverse to be true. We see that as quality increases, so does productivity.

- As defects decrease, yield increases.
- Making it right the first time eliminates rejects and rework.
- Placing responsibility for quality on the operator removes the need for inspection. An operator is indoctrinated to accept full responsibility for quality in his or her work.

These same concepts apply to the purchasing operation.

- As rejections decrease, costs of procurement decrease, as do delays in production.
- A correctly placed purchase order eliminates renegotiation, changes, and rejections.
- Purchasing agents and buyers are indoctrinated to accept responsibility for quality along with price and delivery. Quality is not viewed as the responsibility of "someone else."

Some executives see productivity as increased output for a given input. Too often, the output is measured at the end of the production line, or at the shipping dock. This concept of productivity fails to adequately consider quality. In its broadest sense, the measure of productivity must count only good quality products which meet the customer needs. A manager cannot say a productivity goal was achieved if products are later returned by customers or a product recall occurs due to product deficiencies.

A supplier's view of productivity is one measure of his quality program and serves as a good indicator of what might be expected in products he supplies. Those companies recognizing that improvement of productivity is a by-product of quality improvement are more likely to supply products meeting requirements.

Products meeting requirements are more likely to come from companies that are concerned with long-range goals. Some companies place greater emphasis on short-term objectives, especially earnings. In introducing objectives of improved quality, they are likely to expect results too soon and too easily. Achievement of in-house quality and quality in suppliers' items occurs only over time; it takes patience as well as skill.

Some companies that have been hit hardest by Japanese competitors, such as manufacturers of automobiles and TV sets, have adopted concepts and strategies popularized by the Japanese. Many firms that are not yet affected may still be too complacent about quality. It has been pointed out by the quality experts that the Japanese effort was a nationwide effort over a fifteen- to twenty-year period. U.S. companies trying to incorporate these concepts may find that it takes longer than a few months or even years to achieve improved quality.

THE PURCHASING FUNCTION

Many companies can be viewed as performing a conversion process. Their function is to convert raw materials, parts and/or components (subassemblies) into a product of greater value. For some U.S. companies the procured items and materials constitute more than half the worth of the shipped products. This significant portion of the firm's wealth comes under the control of the purchasing department or purchasing agent. It becomes very important that the procured items meet the quality and schedule requirements at the right price. If these objectives are met, the purchasing operation contributes to the overall profitability of the company.

> *Case Example.* A supplier was providing a mechanical part that had tight tolerances and critical processing techniques. The parts provided by the supplier were out of tolerance for various reasons and could not be used. Consequently, a production line was shut down. A team including the buyer, a quality engineer, a product engineer, and a tool expert visited the supplier's plant. During the visit, various corrective actions were suggested and agreed to by the supplier management, but were not subsequently corrected. A second visit by the same team resulted in additional commitments, and the establishment of a sorting operation at incoming inspection to find defective parts. Nevertheless, the problem was eventually solved only by changing suppliers.

In order to assure the continuity of a company's production operations, it is essential that the right quantity and quality of procured parts and materials be available when needed for the manufacturing process. Shut-down production lines are costly to the company in several ways. Loss of profits, layoff of personnel, and failure to meet the customers' delivery dates are serious problems and may lead to loss of sales. While we can, of course, build up inventories of procured material, it is costly to tie up capital in large inventories, and this course will not be tolerated by management. Besides, material held in inventory sometimes deteriorates or becomes obsolete due to design changes.

Some U.S. automotive manufacturers, as well as many Japanese firms, have introduced JIT (just-in-time) procurement, wherein supplier items are delivered directly to the production line, and no inventories are maintained. Schedule requirements are provided to the purchasing agent by the production department, and the purchasing agent passes the requirements on to the supplier as part of the subcontract. Similarly, product requirements are defined by engineering and become part of the subcontract. The quality control department may specify additional requirements to assure that the product user's needs are achieved. These quality control requirements, just like the engineering requirements, should also become part of the subcontract. The purchasing department must assure that the supplier is capable of meeting all of the standards and is committed to meeting them at competitive costs and on schedule.

In carrying out its responsibilities, the purchasing department interrelates with many other parts of the company. Figure 1-2 illustrates these relationships.

QUALITY AND QUALITY CONTROL

A quality product does not just come about without special effort. Quality control refers to all of the activities that must be

FIG. 1-2. PURCHASING RELATIONSHIPS TO OTHER FUNCTIONS

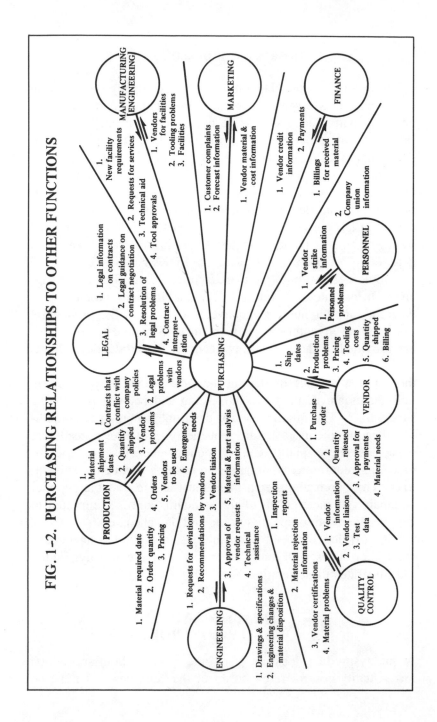

carried out in order to achieve the quality product. Some persons use the concept of a quality program or quality control system in referring to a set of activities that together assure that the product will conform to the standards set for it and thus meet the needs of the user. Quality control represents a broad-based function. There is usually a department called "quality control," but other parts of the company organization also have important roles to perform toward this end.

QUALITY CONTROL
OF PURCHASED MATERIAL

This book relates to quality, quality control, and purchased material. The term purchased material, however, will be used in its broadest sense. It includes raw materials, such as steel stock or chemicals. It includes parts and assembled units often referred to as components. Sometimes these assembled units are operating units such as compressors or motors, to be installed in the final product. Purchased material, as we will use the term, also includes processes. For example, a vendor may be given the task of plating material furnished by the contractor in accordance with a defined process. Services can also be purchased: a vendor may be responsible for product maintenance at a particular location, advertising services, or subcontracted legal services.

Most of the materials mentioned so far are often called hardware, but software can also be purchased from a vendor or supplier. Software usually refers to computer programs, cards, or tapes that are used in relation to product testing or use. It may also refer to the documentation to be maintained by a supplier. Quality of purchased material can refer to any of these, for each can affect the quality of the product shipped to the customer. Any program to control the quality must consider the applicability of each of these to the particular product.

Previously we talked about quality and the quality program or system. This system consisted of activities or tasks that must be carried out to achieve product quality. These activities and standards apply to the vendor, sometimes referred to as a supplier. If the items purchased are complex, the supplier may be called a subcontractor. In any case it is essential, if a product is to possess quality, that the many parts, materials, and processes that make up the product be controlled. It is with these activities related to quality of purchased items that this book will be concerned.

BENEFITS TO A SUPPLIER

A quality program can be imposed on a supplier, but it is much better if the supplier recognizes the importance of quality and initiates an adequate quality program. A quality program can provide several benefits to a supplier: (1) improvement of reputation among customers, (2) reduced costs due to improved quality and reduced rework and defective material, (3) improved marketability of products due to improved quality, (4) improved employee motivation and satisfaction from doing a good job, and (5) increased sales.

When product quality is inadequate, costs increase, schedules are delayed, rework and scrap increases, deliveries are late, productivity declines, and customers are lost. When quality improves and a company has a product better than the competitors, productivity increases, employees are happier, and more customers are gained.

LOOKING AHEAD

In order to compete in today's—and the future's—marketplace, companies have recognized that they must furnish products that the consumer recognizes as desirable in quality and price. Any supplier faces this challenge, because the purchasing organization, as the immediate consumer, has increased the emphasis on these objectives. Thus all members of both organizations must

comprehend the importance of quality and the tie between quality, improved productivity, reduced expenses, and increased sales.
This recognition of importance of quality is enhanced by a strong
commitment from higher levels of management. This concept
appears to be winning a stronger foothold in U.S. companies
prompted by competition from foreign sources.

The remaining chapters of this book deal with quality as part
of strategy in subcontracting; tactical planning and execution by
purchasing to include definition of quality; continuing assess-
ment of quality; and follow-up where necessary to assure that
quality is achieved. Most of these concepts and techniques are
not new—they are tried and proven over many years. We have
found, however, that the integration of these concepts into a
strategy—and its implementation—can provide a basis for a new
look at the total quality-purchasing operation for persons working in these areas.

SPECIFICATION
OF
REQUIREMENTS

Many years ago companies worked under the assumption that engineers designed products and specified requirements, manufacturing built the products, and quality control inspected the product after it was made to assure quality. Beginning in the 1940s, the concept of quality control has gradually evolved into an emphasis on manufacturing quality products that meet the requirements, with only a limited amount of inspection by quality control personnel. The quality control personnel now spend greater effort assuring that quality is built into products and that conformance to requirements is achieved as the products are made.

The same line of reasoning can be applied to the quality relationship with a supplier. The objective is to assure that items or materials provided by a supplier conform to requirements without the need for extensive inspection upon receipt by purchaser. This chapter deals with the approaches to this quality concept and the means of its accomplishment, beginning with the careful definition and specification of requirements.

SPECIFICATIONS AND STANDARDS

Specifications and standards are documents containing criteria that must be met. These consist not only of physical and performance requirements to which the product must conform, but also procedures that must be performed on the equipment—such as tests, material control, reliability verification, etc. In dealing with suppliers, these specifications and standards become part of the purchase order or subcontract and become legally binding documents, as part of the subcontract. They define what is being purchased. Definitions of the commodities to be purchased can also be contained in engineering drawings, catalog descriptions, or other documents.

It is important that each document be incorporated into the purchase order so that there is no doubt that the requirements are part of the subcontract agreement. If a requirement is not stated in the purchase order, there is no basis for enforcing compliance. Many requirements are discussed in the process of source selection and negotiations; some are intentionally discarded as being unnecessary, whereas others become part of the agreed-upon standards.

Standards discussed orally between the buyer and supplier, but never placed in the subcontract or purchase order, often become sources of problems later on. Oral agreements may fail to reach the responsible supplier personnel, or one of the parties may not understand that they are to become part of the final contract agreement.

Actual Case. The requirements for on-time delivery of a critical piece of test equipment were discussed during the negotiation stage with the supplier, but a delivery clause was never placed on the purchase order. Even though the purchase order required status reports against milestones, construction of the equipment was not started until after the delivery date. As a result the equipment was delivered a year late and the buyer was unable to meet his delivery schedule due to inability to test the product.

Agreements along with the related cost must be stated in the purchase order or one of the referenced documents in order to be enforceable.

CONFORMANCE TO
STANDARDS OR REQUIREMENTS

Every product has standards to which it must conform. Product characteristics, dimensions, and process requirements are established by design engineers and are placed on engineering drawings. As the products are produced, measurements are taken using a gauge or other device to determine if the dimensions are within the allowable tolerance. Engineers may also specify performance requirements to be demonstrated. Requirements may also state, for example, that equipment must operate under various environmental conditions, such as at a temperature of 140 degrees Celsius while at a reduced voltage. Product capabilities of this nature can be verified by conducting a test with the equipment operating at that temperature and under the specified load. An endurance test or a life test can also be made on a sample to verify life or reliability specified for the item.

Quality can be defined as conformance to the requirements, and it becomes of utmost importance to assure this conformance. An important part of the manufacturing and quality control function is to assure that the standards and other requirements have been met. Quality control personnel either verify conformance of the product to the standards and specification requirements, or assure that conformance has been verified in the process of manufacture or test.

Establishing controls to assure that quality requirements are met can be viewed as a set of sequential steps.

1. First we identify the needed characteristics and the criticality of each.

2. An appropriate unit of measurement, such as centimeters or volts, is then selected to define each characteristic.

3. Next we establish a standard value and an allowable tolerance for each value.

4. A gauge or test instrument is then chosen that can measure each value.

5. Where appropriate, sampling plans are selected.

6. When the item has been manufactured, the product characteristics are measured.

7. The difference between the product value and the standard or required value is determined.

8. The inspector or tester must next make a decision (i.e., accept or reject) based on the finding.

9. If the product is not acceptable, it is necessary to determine whether the defect could be a random occurrence or attributed to a cause.

10. The final step is to take action as necessary to prevent further occurrence of nonrandom defects.

The concepts of quality control do not require that every dimension or requirement be checked on 100 percent of the items, or even on the sample inspected. In fact, it is better to carry out a task or activity (such as process control) that will assure that products are manufactured correctly to begin with. Most processes can be controlled to assure that defectives are seldom produced. If we are still not sure of the process control, however, samples can be taken and measured for verification as the manufacturing process is carried out. This is much better than producing a large quantity of items and then attempting to determine what percentage are acceptable, or trying to sort the good from the bad parts. With the increasing use of robotics, many processes include automatic devices to perform 100 percent inspection, with an automatic kick-out of rejected items.

WHERE ARE
QUALITY STANDARDS DEFINED?

For purchased commodities, all important characteristics should in some way be specified as part of the purchase agreement. Requirements applying to every item procured by a company can be printed in the standard purchase order form. For example, the phrase "All hazardous materials must be marked" can be part of the "boilerplate requirements" on all purchase orders. Other requirements pertaining to specific commodities or to one item only can be established by the use of engineering specifications, blueprints, physical samples, catalog descriptions, commercial standards, performance specifications, material specifications, drafting standards, or workmanship standards.

In other cases a "general specification" or "supplier specification" may list requirements that apply to all procured products where applicable, such as testing a certain number of items from each lot or furnishing test data to the contractor. Sometimes quality systems specifications or inspection documents are used. Test specifications also describe how tests are to be conducted, frequency of testing, and the required documentation to be prepared from the tests. Frequently an item is described by reference to an industry standard, as for a specific type of steel bar stock or a standard chemical.

ENGINEERING DRAWINGS
(BLUEPRINTS OR PRINTS)

An engineering drawing is a pictorial and/or narrative description of an item, including dimensions and other descriptive information. The dimensions include tolerances and are given in sufficient detail to avoid possible misinterpretation. Use of a common drafting approach (such as ANSI Y 14.5) will eliminate potential interpretation errors. It also provides definitions for terms often misused. In procurement, a company will use drawings showing the supplier in detail exactly how the item is to look. Drawings often describe processes used in the manufacture or treatment of the item, and are frequently used to depict machined parts, castings, fabricated items, forging, or other specially made items.

The manufacturer must know to what revised standards the part must be made, otherwise he cannot be sure he is making the item correctly, nor can the inspector know how to inspect it. It is not uncommon for the purchaser's inspectors to mistakenly use a different revision of a drawing from that used by the supplier in cases where a change is not specified in the purchase order.

When buying according to a drawing (print), the drawing number and revision (plus any applicable changes) must be specified as part of the purchase order. For example, the purchase order may state "Deliver 50 items in accordance with General Co. drawing #400654 Rev. C, and changes 1 through 6." It is intended that the supplier manufacture the items and assure conformance to the drawing before shipment to the purchaser. Upon receipt from the supplier, purchaser's receiving inspection personnel are able to inspect the item against the same drawings with dimensions and other requirements used by the supplier. If the supplier has been selected properly and the requirements stated adequately, the receiving inspection personnel might need only to check the supplier's data and verify its adequacy, and then the material can be delivered directly to production.

When drawings are used, it is the supplier's responsibility to meet the standards, dimensions and tolerances, and other requirements given on the drawing. It is the buying company's (contractor's) responsibility to ensure that the drawings are correct and complete and that the design meets the performance and other end-use needs of the product and its users.

PHYSICAL SAMPLE

In some cases the product to be delivered by the supplier is defined by a physical sample furnished by the contractor. Physical samples are particularly helpful in establishing limits on appearance requirements such as paint splatter density. In this case less descriptive information is necessary. The physical sample is satisfactory as a standard in cases where the item to be furnished is not complicated, and where material content and tolerances are not important. In production of a toy, for example, while a model may be acceptable, it still may be necessary to write some requirements into the purchase order, such as avoidance of sharp edges, loose pieces, or toxic materials. Tolerances are less important as long as the item functions as intended.

Samples may also be used successfully in the purchase of fruits, eggs, or other items in which the quality or size can be compared to samples for grading. It would be difficult, however, for the buyer's receiving inspection department to determine whether a product is identical to a sample if dimensions, tolerances, or material composition of the item are to be verified.

Samples of these types do present problems, however, when they need to be reproduced, especially if the time for it is two or three years later. Samples may also degrade with use and time.

BRAND NAME OR
CATALOG DESCRIPTION

Suppliers often publish catalogs in which their products are described. The catalog could contain either the performance characteristics or other descriptive material. A buyer can then select the desired item based on the catalog description. The catalog could reference product warranties, interchangeability, material composition, or other standards which apply to the item. Selecting a catalog item is one of the simplest methods of specifying the products being produced by a supplier, but there are a number of problems associated with this method. First, it often restricts the procurement to a single supplier, unless the item to be purchased has an industry standard and more than one supplier produces the same item. Furthermore, when there is a single source, the supplier is less likely to negotiate prices. Also, any disruption in the supplier's production, such as a strike or quality problem, may result in manufacturing schedule delays for the purchaser.

In some cases the item purchased by brand name or catalog description is patented, which again restricts the bidding to a single supplier. In cases in which the engineer specifies a brand name, however, the purchasing agent should exercise his authority to seek an alternative similar product that would satisfy the need. If alternative sources are found, the bidding promises to be more competitive, and work disruptions or quality problems at one supplier plant will not disrupt the contractor's production.

One of the main drawbacks of ordering by brand name or catalog number is the difficulty in determining what characteristics to inspect or test at receiving inspection. The design engineer or quality engineer can, however, furnish the receiving inspection personnel with information on the important characteristics.

Problems can also arise due to the control of a proprietary design by the vendor. For example, the buying company may have been using a catalog part for a long time and found it satisfactory. The supplier, perhaps wanting to improve the product, then makes a change in the design or in a material, which does not affect the catalog description. All of a sudden the using company experiences a problem. After considerable time and effort it determines that the new material used by the supplier becomes distorted in the user's application. The supplier had not realized that the change in design or material would affect the usability by a customer. This type of problem occurs frequently, since it is not easy for a supplier to be fully aware of all uses of each product, and sometimes the use involves unusual environments where moisture, heat, or cold are present.

COMMERCIAL STANDARDS

Purchasing to commercial standards provides many advantages to both the using company and the supplier. Sometimes these are industry standards, developed by a particular group such as the electrical industries. In other cases they are national standards. Sheet steel, screws, pipe, chemicals, lubricating oil, and many electrical parts are normally purchased in this way. When buying according to commercial standards, the purchasing department can easily request competitive bids and select the supplier offering the lowest price. There is complete clarity as to exactly what is wanted and needed. A commercial standard cannot be changed by the supplier alone, and each party knows exactly what inspections or tests can be performed. Usually, the parts or material can be obtained quickly because they are carried in a supplier's inventory.

Control of quality upon receipt of the shipment may be more difficult. The commercial standard may list some characteristics easily inspected, whereas other characteristics such as strength or material content are not easily verified. In general, however, this method of purchasing should cause the least number of quality difficulties as long as the user's application is correct.

There are some disadvantages to using commercial standards. Since the commodities are used in many applications, the purchaser's ability to define his or her special needs is limited. A special need, such as burr-free edge material, generally requires modification of the commercial standard.

Case Example. A timing belt used in a complex electronics device was specified by use of a commercial standard. The electronics device experienced intermittent defects which were traced to flash on the timing belt.

The flash, however, met the requirements of the commercial specification. In order to resolve this problem, the design engineer issued a special specification to require the removal of the flash before use of the timing belts.

Sometimes a commercial standard is mentioned in the supplier's catalog or on the goods themselves. An example is UL, meaning approved by Underwriter's Laboratory. In other cases products will indicate conformance to certain federal agency requirements, such as those of the Food and Drug Administration (FDA). There are many of these, but there is no assurance that these stipulations will satisfy a particular user's needs. It is very helpful, however, for the information to be available to persons performing inspections and tests.

PERFORMANCE SPECIFICATIONS

A performance specification describes what an item is required to do and under what conditions. For example, a 2 HP, 1,800 RPM motor is described as being able to operate with a certain torque at −40 to 120 degrees Celsius. The supplier of the motor is free to determine how the performance is to be achieved, by selecting the size, weight, or type of the motor. In other cases a specification describes the exact physical size and mounting and how the purchased item fits with other parts of the final product, and it may specify dimensions, weight limits, or other characteristics. The specification may also state exactly how the item is to be tested or it may state any other method by which the performance is to be verified. Performance specifications may be used when the purchaser lacks knowledge about the design of the part or does not care about the construction of the item and is primarily interested in its function. They are particularly useful in specifying products that perform a function, such as software. The engineer is willing to leave the design details up to the supplier, as long as the necessary functions can be performed.

The use of performance specifications gives the supplier substantial freedom in design of the item, provided the performance is achieved. The supplier will be able to take advantage of up-to-date methods or materials, or can use patented items. Therefore, the purchasing company using performance specifications may expect to obtain lower bids from suppliers than it would if the design were exactly defined. In any type of procurement, if a company is restricted to only one supplier, the company should ascertain the credibility of the supplier and should examine alternatives. Some suppliers tend to promote their more expensive products when a less expensive item would suffice.

COMMODITIES STANDARDS

Developing specifications for each type of commodity will result in consistent quality requirements. A typical company's commodities listing might be as follows:

ADHESIVES	CONNECTORS, CONTACTS
ALUMINUM	COPPER
BATTERIES	CRT DISPLAYS
BEARINGS	CRYSTALS
BELTS	ELECTRONIC COMPONENTS
BLOWERS	ENGINEERING SUPPLIES
CABLE	FABRICATED PARTS, ASSYS
CAPACITORS	FANS
CAPITAL EQUIPMENT	FIBRE, PHENOLIC PARTS
CARBON PRODUCTS	FUSES
CASTINGS	GAUGES
CHEMICALS	GASKETS
CLUTCHES	GEARS
COILS	GLASS PRODUCTS
COMPUTER ITEMS	HARDWARE

HOUSEHOLD MOVES

INTEGRATED CIRCUITS

LAMPS

LUBRICANTS, OILS

MACHINED PARTS

MAGNETS

MAINTENANCE & REPAIR

MOTORS

NAMEPLATES

OFFICE EQUIPMENT/SUPPLIES

PACKAGING MATERIALS

PAINTS

PAPER PRODUCTS

PLASTIC

PLUMBING SUPPLIES

POWER SUPPLIES

PRINTED WIRE BOARDS

PRINTING SUPPLIES

RELAYS, SOLENOIDS

RESISTORS

RIBBON, PRINT

RUBBER PARTS

SAFETY EQUIPMENT

SERVICE CONTRACTS

SHOP SUPPLIES

SLEEVING

SOCKETS

SOLDER

SPRINGS

STAMPINGS

STEEL

SWITCHES

TAPES

TOOLS

TRANSFORMERS

VARISTORS

WIRE

MATERIAL SPECIFICATIONS

Companies often prepare material specifications for use in ordering from suppliers because they provide control over the exact makeup of the purchased material or item. A material specification lists the composition of the desired material or otherwise describes its chemical and physical properties. Typical purchases are raw materials, lubricants, liquids, paints, or other substances. How can the material be checked upon receipt from the supplier? Normally an analysis can be performed to verify the composition of the material. In some cases controls are established at the supplier's facility to ascertain that the composition is sufficiently controlled during the processing. The supplier then furnishes test reports or certification of compliance.

There are advantages and disadvantages in using material specifications. When material specifications are used, the buyer assumes a greater responsibility for quality. As long as the supplier furnishes the material in accordance with specification, it is the buyer's responsibility to make sure that the material as described will meet the end-use needs. An additional disadvantage is that the buyer who uses his or her own material specifications may not be aware of recently developed materials that may perform equally well at a lower price, or provide better performance at the same price.

Once the buyer runs a qualification test on the supplier's material, there can be reasonable assurance that the supplier will not make changes if the purchase order calls out the material specification. In the absence of specifications in the purchase order, a supplier may make improvements in processes or designs. Since the supplier is not aware of exactly how all of the customers use the material, the process change might result in adverse effects as used by a particular customer.

WORKMANSHIP STANDARDS

The lack of workmanship standards can result in the fabrication of parts that meet the basic requirements, but do not function properly, are unreliable, or have an unacceptable appearance. Workmanship standards include, but are not limited to: quality of solder joints, definition of burrs, breakaway, concentricity, flatness, squareness, surface roughness, characteristics of welds, wire wraps, flash, taper, blow holes, crazing, coloration, appearance, etc. The degree to which each of these is defined is dependent on the product application and criticality. The appearance of a refrigerator door may prevent its eventual sale even though it will not affect its function. A poor solder joint or weld joint may result in a reliability failure of an airplane, pressure vessel, etc. Establishing required workmanship standards in advance of negotiation will aid in minimizing misunderstandings and problems.

> *Actual Case.* The appearance of a unit was discussed during negotiation but never documented in a meaningful fashion. When produced, it had a good appearance but the wrong color. Further negotiation resulted in rework of the unit to the right general color, but it still did not match, since no tolerance on color had been established. Additional definition and more costly rework eventually resulted in an acceptable product. The extra cost and delay would have been avoided with an appropriate, documented workmanship standard for appearance.

CONTENT OF SPECIFICATIONS
AND STANDARDS

While specifications used in the procurement of products or materials usually are similar in format, the length and detail of the various parts of the specification can vary considerably. The company acting as custodian of the specification will be named on the document along with the engineer or others responsible for its preparation and maintenance. The responsible engineer will prepare and maintain the document in accordance with format and change procedures established by the company. Sometimes the supplier, if a sole source of procurement, will be named in the specification. In other cases alternate sources of supply may be listed. Listing of suppliers in the specification gives guidance to the purchasing agent, but also limits the agent's ability to secure other sources from which purchases can be made. Listing the supplier's name may also necessitate revision of the document whenever a new supplier is located or an old supplier is to be removed.

The specification will contain the product name and a specification number in accordance with the company's standard numbering procedure. The applicable revision letter and any changes incorporated will also be given on each drawing or specification. The product or material description and/or performance requirements make up a substantial part of the specification. Sometimes drawings or other process or test specifications are referenced and become part of the specification requirements. The document may describe the performance of the product, give detailed dimensions, set power consumption requirements, set noise or environmental restrictions, establish minimum safety requirements, or specify materials to be used. In any case there must be sufficient description so that there is no question as to exactly what is to be furnished by the supplier.

Dimensions, characteristics, or defects may also be classified as to their importance. Possible defects that are life threatening, such as the release of a toxic substance, and requirements important to the functioning of the product are identified as much more serious than characteristics that affect appearance only. All of these characteristics, along with tolerances, are often referred to as quality characteristics.

The specification also describes the ways in which the requirements are to be verified and establishes criteria for final acceptance. Qualification tests prove that the design of the product will perform as required. They are usually performed before many items are built. However, sometimes parts are periodically requalified. Acceptance tests or inspections are performed on each unit, or on a sample of the units from each lot. A sampling plan may be included as part of the specification.

Finally, the specification will contain information as to how the item is to be packaged, along with any prescribed methods of handling, shipping, or storage. It may also include requirements for labeling, restrictions on storage life, or other storage conditions allowed or not allowed. Operating and maintenance procedures are usually given in other separate documents, such as handbooks.

ENVIRONMENTAL REQUIREMENTS

Products are used under varied conditions. A part used in a freezer needs a different set of standards than a part used in a washing machine or one used in an airplane. Extreme temperature, pressure, humidity, and shock are examples of use conditions. The conditions under which the performance and other standards must be met are often called the "environmental requirements." Before deciding that a part furnished by a supplier will perform in the necessary environment, the engineer will review the catalog information prepared by the supplier, or confer with the supplier about the needed performance. At some point the engineer will want to see test results proving that the part will perform as claimed, and may decide that special tests are to be performed by either the supplier or himself. These tests are called qualification tests and include tests under the specified environmental conditions. When the tests are completed satisfactorily, it can be stated that the item has been qualified. It is part of the purchasing agent's responsibility to make sure that supplied items have been qualified before orders are placed for production quantities.

SPECIFICATIONS:
PROS AND CONS

The use of specifications has several advantages to the company buying the purchased items or materials. Initially it means that the engineer has to carefully think through the exact needs and the requirements to be specified. If this is done well, it removes or reduces the likelihood of future misunderstandings due to lack of clarity or inadequate definition of dimensions, standards, or other specified requirements. A company will usually want two or more suppliers of the identical item. The use of a detailed specification will help assure that items obtained from any of the sources will be identical and interchangeable. However, care must be taken to assure that process variations do not affect the interchangeability. For example, a rolled thread and cut thread may meet the same specification but perform differently.

When a specification is used in procurement, it is easier to secure competitive bids from several potential suppliers. Each bidder and the contracting company can be sure that each supplier is bidding on the same thing. Each supplier will be aware of exactly what is needed, and can be assured that every other bidder is pricing the identical item. The increased competition in the bidding process is likely to result in a lower price being negotiated with the successful bidder, and in less risk that the product will fail to meet requirements.

When the completed product is eventually received by the receiving inspection department, the specifications and drawings can be used to verify that all standards are—or are not—met. The supplier quality control personnel will have had the same documents to work with, a fact that should reduce the possibilities of disagreement on whether requirements are met.

PRODUCT USE INFORMATION

By human nature, a person who understands how a particular item is to be used and why certain requirements are important will probably exert more care in the job. Experience has also shown that educating workers about the product results in improvements in workmanship and quality. This concept can be extended to supplier personnel. Some companies send out teams to the supplier plant to survey the plant and to inform its supplier personnel about the problems that exist when specified requirements are not being met. Similarly, if supplier manufacturing personnel visit the contractor's plant and see exactly how the supplier items are used, perhaps there will be greater understanding and acceptance of the actual need for each of the specified requirements. Otherwise, they may see the requirements only as an abstract group of standards.

From a higher management point of view, if the manager of the supplier plant came into the user's plant and saw a production line shut down because of defective parts, perhaps the importance of each standard would be appreciated and attention to the problem would be greater.

There is, of course, another side to the product use information coin. Sometimes a contractor will specify tolerances tighter than actually necessary. If supplier personnel find this to be true on some occasions, it may result in careless treatment of all requirements, to the detriment of both supplier and contractor. Working closely with a supplier in the early stages of a contract can help a contractor eliminate unneeded requirements and reduce costs. If the supplier is invited to submit his suggestions at the time of the original bidding or negotiation, a more satisfactory product description can be arrived at. Suppliers often hesitate to make suggestions during the original bidding or negotiations for fear of being judged noncompliant or incapable of meeting the specified requirements. This is, however, the best time to identify unnecessarily stringent requirements and arrive at standards that will meet the needs of the final product and also be within the capability of the supplier's manufacturing facility.

A supplier also has some implied legal and moral responsibility to provide goods suitable to the purpose for which they are to be used. This is particularly true when the final product is a commercial item such as a washing machine, iron, etc. This responsibility may even extend beyond the exact standards specified. If the supplier has not, however, been advised of the end-use purpose, and the items later turn out to be unsuitable for the intended use, the purchasing company has no recourse against the supplier.

A fully informed supplier will probably go out of his or her way to help the contractor. If a potential supplier does make suggestions for revised requirements, and the ideas are accepted by the buying company, the specification or purchase order must incorporate the changes. This, however, still does not relieve the purchasing company of responsibility in the event of future problems related to the suggestion. Neither can a purchasing agent just leave it up to the supplier to furnish a usable product. The purchasing agent still has the primary responsibility to management, and will be held responsible in case problems occur later. Therefore, the purchasing agent should take the lead in providing an atmosphere for cooperation between supplier and contractor throughout the procurement process.

VALIDITY OF STANDARDS

A standard that is too lax may result in a product that will not perform as needed. It could also cause the product to lack sufficient life or reliability or to fail to work correctly with other parts in the finished product. Incorrect tolerances, for example, may result in items that do not fit together properly with other parts.

Standards that are too stringent may cause costs to be greater than necessary, possibly resulting in a product not competitive in price. Higher prices of supplied items, because of unnecessarily stringent standards, can result in reduced company profits.

Standards must be valid—that is, neither too lax nor too stringent. Validity can be affected by inaccuracy or incompleteness of the requirements; lack of clarity; omission of recent design changes; failure to use up-to-date materials, parts, or processes; or the omission of applicable customer requirements. Also to be avoided are inconsistent standards, incomplete descriptions, and ambiguous statements. In addition to these considerations, it is important to define the method of verification of each requirement. The test equipment and testing sequence used by the supplier should be nondamaging to the product and compatible with that used by the contractor. This necessity of compatibility also applies to calibration, gauges, other methods of measurement, and conditions under which tests are conducted. Problems in any of these factors can result in a lack of valid standards.

CLEAR COMMUNICATION OF REQUIREMENTS

Standards involve interpretation. Many quality problems arise between vendors and contractors because the supplier makes an interpretation of a standard that is different from the interpretation of the contractor. The following illustrate some of the communication problem areas.

TERMS AND DEFINITIONS

Terms such as ''smooth surface'' or ''no scratches'' are insufficient as quality standards unless each of these terms is clearly defined. While a hairline scratch may be acceptable, there is probably some depth at which the scratch becomes unacceptable. A degree of surface smoothness acceptable for some applications may be unacceptable for others. Where these or similar terms are used, an agreement must be reached as to the exact definition. These definitions, when agreed upon, should then be documented as part of the design drawings or specifications and thus become part of the purchase order.

JUDGMENTS AND TOLERANCES

Tolerances on dimensions are usually easy to define, since they are measurable. In other cases involving characteristics such as color, roughness, or purity of a liquid, there is less precision and it becomes more difficult to have a clear standard. Samples or pictures may be helpful to clarify the criteria, but it is important that both supplier and contractor use identical samples when they perform their inspections. Sometimes it is useful to prepare physical models showing acceptable and unacceptable conditions. Unusual curves and shapes are often difficult to describe in words, so use of identical, duplicate models by the supplier and contractor can reduce the number of cases in which the supplier judges the item to be acceptable while the contractor rejects it. Developing standards showing the extremes of all acceptable conditions is difficult since the extremes of individual items may be acceptable but the extremes of all combinations may not.

Both the supplier and the contractor are interested in avoiding conflicts or differences of opinion. Even though one of the parties may win out in a particular disagreement, any controversy is costly to both parties in terms of time, money, and trust. The supplier has the natural desire to satisfy the customer. However, there is a limit to what can be done in order to provide this satisfaction. On items already shipped or manufactured, any changes or remaking can be costly. Both supplier and contractor have profit as one of their management objectives.

Many companies have standard manufacturing practices, workmanship standards, design standards, or lists of standard parts for their products. It would not normally be expected that the standards of a supplier and the contractor are identical. If, in the negotiating phase of a subcontract, the supplier and the contractor exchange copies of their standards, each can review the other's for differences and potential problems. A supplier normally sells to many customers, and each customer might have a set of standards, sometimes with differing requirements. It may be difficult for the vendor to have to meet the diverse needs of several customers. However, this interchange of information with each customer early in the negotiating phase will help both the supplier and contractor. Whereas minor differences might easily be resolved, some serious differences may suggest the selection of a different supplier. Some companies also have quality control practices or procedures. Exchanging information on these standards early in the negotiating stage is also helpful in avoiding problems later.

PROCUREMENT OF SERVICES

Establishing requirements in the procurement of services is just as important as in the purchase of goods, but the need is not always as apparent to the buyer.

Services can be grouped into three categories: (1) *technical services,* such as software development, service manuals, or maintenance, (2) *professional services,* such as engineering, legal, or consulting services, and (3) *operating services,* such as a food service, janitorial services, or grounds maintenance. For any of these types of services, many firms use a "statement of work," which defines the work to be accomplished, preferably in terms of the end result desired. Since quality has been defined as conformance to requirements—or conformance to customer needs—a means is needed to measure how well the service has been accomplished. When feasible, the fee paid for the service can depend on the degree of conformance to the requirements or objectives.

STANDARDS, PRACTICES, AND POLICY

Some companies take the view that standards, including tolerances, should be somewhat tighter than actually necessary for product functions or performance. The reasoning might be that there will be leeway in case items received are outside of the tolerance. This practice tends to become a company philosophy of tolerances tighter than necessary, but loosely enforced. This concept rarely provides productive results for either the company or its suppliers. Experience has shown that in the long run it is better to specify realistic standards and tolerances and enforce them rigidly. In later chapters of this book we will deal with deviations from requirements that might be accepted for use. However, this should not suggest that a company establish the practice of relaxing requirements, nor of accepting out-of-tolerance items on a regular basis. The best policy is to set standards that are needed, can be met by the supplier, can be verified, are not meant to be relaxed, and are enforced except in unusual circumstances. If an out-of-tolerance item is accepted, a plan of corrective action should be taken to prevent further occurrence. However, if an out-of-tolerance condition can be accepted with no effect on performance, reliability, or appearance, a specification revision should be made.

SPECIFICATION REVIEW

A specification contains the detailed requirements that a product must meet. From the viewpoint of the purchasing department, there are two categories of specifications. In one case the entire specification describes a product to be procured from a supplier. In the second case the product described by the specification is to be manufactured in-house, but some of the materials and parts called out in the specification are to be procured from suppliers. The specification review applies to both situations. It is a systematic procedure in which various functional groups of the company—such as production, tooling, manufacturing, engineering, quality control, testing, and purchasing—examine the specification, usually prior to its formal issuance. Quality control personnel demand clarity of requirements and the ability to make checks and tests of the dimensions, tolerances, and other characteristics. The purchasing representative checks for available sources of supply, necessary lead time, and price. Suggestions for alternative materials and parts are important contributions of the buyer.

Where purchased parts and materials are involved, it is usually necessary for purchasing to make contacts with potential suppliers in order to secure answers to important questions. Are the items readily available, or will they have to be specially made? Are tolerances realistic? The questions asked should provide answers to both quality and economic considerations. The potential suppliers are often asked to look over a specification to help answer these questions. Any agreed-upon changes can then be incorporated prior to the signing of the subcontract agreement.

CHANGE CONTROL

The control of design changes is sometimes called "configuration management." The word *configuration* refers to an item and the particular drawing or specification changes that apply. An item made according to revision *A* would be of a different configuration than one made to revision *B*, even though most people could not readily see a difference. Likewise, an item made to revision *B* and change No. 1 would be of a still different configuration. The term *configuration management* refers to a systematic set of procedures for identification, control, and accounting for the design changes. The objective is to make sure that the correct changes are reflected in each piece of equipment and to have records to show which changes are incorporated into any particular equipment. The concept of configuration management originated in defense procurement and applies mainly to complex equipment. An individual product may be subjected to a configuration audit to ascertain exactly which design changes have been incorporated into it.

Change control applies to all procured items. It is important to know exactly which drawing changes have been incorporated in any item. The purchasing agent has an important role in the change control procedure and in making it work so that the configuration of any item can be determined. The purchase order should specify the revision to which the item is being purchased.

QUALITY CONTROL
RESPONSIBILITIES FOR
SPECIFICATIONS

Engineering personnel are generally responsible for the preparation and content of specifications. This does not mean that quality control personnel have unimportant responsibilities, however. The best procedure is to allow quality control people to review supplier specifications when they are initially prepared and also when any revision or change is proposed. The quality control or test personnel can often make suggestions related to the following:

1. More effective test methods
2. Sampling plan usage
3. Difficulties in checking certain characteristics with available gauges
4. The newest measuring techniques
5. Clarification of requirements where there might be more than one interpretation
6. Requirements or dimensions where no method of verification is given
7. Tolerances difficult to meet on existing manufacturing equipment
8. Clarification of the relative importance of requirements, or the degree of verification needed for each requirement

Identification and resolution of any of these potential problems in the review can prevent later problems with the supplier.

RESPONSIBILITIES OF
THE PURCHASING AGENT
FOR QUALITY

A purchasing agent is responsible for all aspects of a procurement—including schedule, cost, and quality of the material procured. When a specification is given to a supplier for bidding purposes or as part of a subcontract, the supplier often has questions on interpretation. Suppliers may also make suggestions for changes in the specification. The purchasing agent acts as a go-between for the supplier and the engineer who prepared the specification. It is usually not sufficient to pass along the questions and the answers. Where something can be interpreted in more than one way, the purchasing agent should demand that the specification be changed so that it can be interpreted in only one way. If a change is to be made in specifications of an existing subcontract, all bidders, or multiple suppliers, should have a chance to see the change and comment on the possible effects. Problems could result if changes are not given to all affected suppliers for review prior to actual implementation.

QUALITY REQUIREMENTS
VS.
TYPE OF SUBCONTRACT

Various types of contracts and their effects on quality and quality control are discussed in a later chapter. At this time it is appropriate, however, to mention that there is a relationship between the type of contract and the firmness of the quality requirements. With the firm fixed-price contract, the supplier bids on exact requirements. It is expected that there will be little variance from these requirements in later negotiation, unless there is a suggestion for improvement or a change needed to correct a deficiency in the product.

In other cases, both the supplier and the contractor recognize that the specification requirements are subject to change, possibly because they are not complete, because the product is in the development stage, or for other reasons. As a result, the buyer may utilize either a fixed-price redeterminable or cost reimbursement contract. These two types of contracts are recognized as being more likely to undergo requirements, schedule, and price changes subsequent to their signing. A change in quality requirements could result in a schedule change and/or price adjustment.

NEGOTIATING
QUALITY REQUIREMENTS
WITH A SUPPLIER

In some procurements the specifications and requirements are sent out to the potential suppliers for bids. When the successful bidder has been identified, there will still be some matters to negotiate before it can be said that the subcontractor has been firmly selected. In other procurements one supplier may be selected for negotiation without going through the bidding process. The negotiation phase provides an opportunity for the contractor and the supplier to carefully go over all of the terms of the specifications, drawings, and other documents included in the purchase order.

One objective is to assure a common understanding of the standards and requirements, including quality requirements. Whenever any dual interpretations arise, there is an opportunity to make the clarification and place the clear definition in the contractual documents. Suggestions by either party for doing something in a less expensive way or in a manner that will improve performance or product life or reliability can also be considered in the negotiation process. The bargaining on the quality aspects is done concurrently with bargaining on schedule, price, and other factors over which there are differences of opinion. These factors are not independent since changes in quality standards may affect price or delivery dates. The interrelationships are not always obvious, and a considerable amount of judgment and intuition is involved. In the negotiation process, some of the quality characteristics will be flexible whereas others will have little or no room for change—depending on their relationship to product function, reliability, safety, etc.

Some people view the negotiations as a situation in which the buyer is trying to get the price down and the seller trying to get it higher. In reality, it is not so simple. All of the factors—including schedule, price, and quality—interrelate and must be considered together. Bidding on standard items involves the least negotiation; procurement of one-of-a-kind items involves the most.

Prior to entering into negotiation with a supplier, a purchasing agent will usually develop a strategy for the company. From the above considerations, it is apparent that engineering, quality, and scheduling personnel should all be involved in the process. All of them, however, need not always be present in the meeting with the supplier negotiating team. Having the quality expert on call is often an effective way of proceeding. The negotiating strength of the buyer will depend on several factors. Is there more than one available supplier? Has the buyer taken steps implying that a subcontractual arrangement already exists with one supplier? The purchasing agent who has developed alternate suppliers and has laid out strategy is in a better position to negotiate favorably for the company.

Those involved in the negotiation should carefully prepare for it. The quality and purchasing people should be familiar with the specifications, the items being procured, and their use in the final product, even though most of these types of technical questions will be directed toward the engineer. Without knowledge of the more important and less important characteristics, the quality representative will have difficulty in responding to suggestions or requested changes from the supplier's negotiating team. There should always be a designated leader of the negotiating team to assure the presentation of a unified position on each item negotiated.

In preparation for the negotiation, specific objectives should be established. Objectives like "getting all we can" are of little value. Setting limits on price and schedule, and the identification of critical quality characteristics are more important factors.

SUMMARY OF PURCHASING STRATEGY TO ACHIEVE REQUIREMENTS

Strategy is an overall plan by a company to achieve its objectives. We have stated that purchasing has responsibilities regarding quality, schedule, and price. The purchasing department has alternative ways to achieve these objectives. Some of these alternatives are as follows:

1. Use multiple sources or provide for alternative sources so that the company does not become dependent upon one source of supply. Obtain competitive bids or price quotations.
2. Concentrate on fewer suppliers, but take steps to assure they will be long-term, quality suppliers.
3. Evaluate sources of supply prior to placing orders based on past performance and upon capabilities observed during visits to the supplier facility.
4. Define all of the essential or helpful information carefully in each subcontract and purchase order so that the supplier fully comprehends the requirements and is given the clear responsibility to meet them.
5. Withhold payments to suppliers until there is reasonable assurance that products received meet the requirements.

6. Evaluate the received material as soon as possible after receipt. Make acceptance conditional if certain requirements cannot be verified at that time.
7. Require the supplier to furnish evidence with the material showing that the requirements have been met. This evidence could be test or inspection reports.
8. Visit the supplier's facility to inspect or verify the status of material prior to shipments to the contractor.
9. Establish good working relationships with suppliers.
10. Educate the supplier on the requirements and why they are really important in the use of the end product.
11. Research the financial stability of each potential supplier.
12. Define procedures in the subcontract for handling design changes without excessive costs or delays.
13. Provide technical assistance to vendors when they request assistance or do not have the capability to solve their quality problems.

SUPPLIER
EVALUATION AND
SELECTION

The process of purchasing requires the selection of a supplier. One of the best ways to obtain the right quality in purchased goods is to select a supplier who has the competence to do the job. For the purchase to be satisfactory, it is important to select a supplier who is capable of meeting the quality requirements and with whom agreement on price and schedule can be reached. These things cannot happen without careful planning and without the exercise of professional skills. Sometimes the source selection process involves selecting the best supplier from among several capable prospects. In other situations source selection becomes a matter of finding a capable source who can meet the requirements. In still other cases a capable source may not be located and purchasing is faced with the task of developing one.

STEPS IN SOURCE SELECTION

The first step in source selection is the identification of possible suppliers, sometimes called the ''bid base.'' For some procurements the purchasing department will be aware of possible suppliers. In other cases the need for a supplier is generated by the need for a product or material not previously purchased. In some of these situations the question will be ''Who makes the item?''

Where no supplier is found, the question becomes "Who might be able to make the item?" Searching through catalogs, trade journals, or directories may be the starting point. Data from catalogs or qualified parts lists can help in determining whether the requirements can be met by a particular supplier.

The second step in supplier selection is to evaluate the possible sources and identify those who are capable and acceptable sources. Capability requires adequate facilities, technical know-how, and competence to achieve quality. Acceptability relates to financial stability, production and engineering competence, interest in doing business with one's company, managerial competence, and willingness to cooperate. From the quality viewpoint, it is also necessary to consider quality capabilities for future production quantity needs. The resources needed to produce a few quality items in a job shop are different from the resources necessary to produce quality under higher rates of production. In the evaluation phase the relative qualifications of suppliers are compared and the advantages and disadvantages of each are considered. Experience of a supplier is an important element affecting quality. It is often desirable to select two or three sources to reduce risks and to help assure future price competition. Although the purchasing agent or buyer might rely to a great extent on the quality control department to evaluate the quality competence of a supplier, the buyer cannot completely delegate this responsibility. Purchasing has the records on suppliers' past performance, transmits all documentation to the supplier, and is the official communication channel with the supplier. We might say, then, that the purchasing agent or buyer is in charge of the procurement and bears the primary responsibility for its success or for any problems that later arise.

ALTERNATIVE SUPPLIERS

Frequently an engineer will design a product using an available part from a particular supplier. This is often necessary in order to find something that will perform as required and will meet the environmental and use conditions. In this case, when the buyer receives the bill of materials, it will list the part, showing the particular manufacturer and perhaps the catalog number. Although it may be purchasing department policy to avoid the use of single sources, the buyer in this situation will probably have no immediate alternative but the single source. Even if the material list specifies "or equal," the buyer has difficulty in ascertaining what will actually be of equal performance and quality.

The proper procedure in this case is for the buyer to seek one or more alternative items and have these suppliers submit performance characteristics or test data for the design engineer to evaluate. If any of the alternative products prove to be satisfactory, they can be added to the bill of materials. This will allow the buyer to obtain competitive bids, and also to have backups in case one of the suppliers is unable to deliver on schedule due to a strike, a quality problem is encountered, or other problems occur with one supplier. In some situations the buyer may purchase from two or more sources on a continuing basis, which assures that more than one supplier is always geared up to furnish the item.

When parts or materials from two or more sources are used as "equals," it is necessary to assure their *interchangeability,* which means that either part can be used in the final product without noticeable difference in performance or need for adjustment. In order to ascertain this it may be necessary to determine the variability of particular characteristics. Two brands of resistors, for example, may have the same mean resistance and be built to the same tolerances, but the distribution of one may be skewed. If the final product were adjusted to the skewed distribution, the other brand might not perform as well in the product. These types of variability problems can also result from temperature or humidity variations under use. Although two parts may appear to be identical, they would not be truly interchangeable for a particular use.

LIMITED NUMBER OF SUPPLIERS

In the early 1980s many companies recognized the advantages of limiting the number of suppliers. The basic idea was that if a supplier knows that he will have business over an extended number of years—as long as quality is maintained—the supplier will plan accordingly, and be willing to spend more to develop and provide long-term quality at lower costs. General Motors refers to this concept of developing long-term agreements as life-cycle procurement.

Companies using this concept feel that the development of vendors who can supply good quality items requires a great deal of personal attention, but is worth the effort. If a supplier can be convinced to make the needed investment to improve processes and productivity, lower costs and improved quality will result. The concept takes advantage of supplier know-how and talent as related to the supplier's own product. Many companies enter into long-term contracts with suppliers. Prior to the 1960s a one-year contract with a supplier was considered to be long-term. Today contracts up to five years are becoming common practice. By the summer of 1983, a Ford executive estimated that between 15 and 20 percent of the dollar value of his company's purchases were under contracts for three or more years.

The end result of this trend is for a company to rely on fewer suppliers, and sometimes a single source for a particular part. In the past, a sole source supplier was often considered a mistake. This concept of fewer suppliers allows the company to allocate resources more carefully and to concentrate on those suppliers who are more promising.

SUPPLIER EVALUATION

The evaluation of a supplier can be divided into two parts. One is the product evaluation and the other is the evaluation of the supplier's ability.

It must first be determined whether the supplier's product is able to meet the design requirements specified—unless, of course, it is a new product yet to be developed. This phase may involve review of test data from the supplier to see whether the product qualifies and meets all standards. Sometimes one or more parts will be ordered from potential suppliers so that the buyer's engineering department or quality department can actually run its own qualification tests. These may include reliability, life, and environmental tests.

The second part of the evaluation is to determine whether the supplier can deliver goods that will conform to all requirements over the span of the contract. In other words, is the supplier able to manufacture conforming products in production quantities? While this phase of the evaluation is more difficult, past experience is one measure of this ability. An evaluation of the supplier's procedures, policies, facilities, and people is necessary to determine the ability to supply quality products.

FIXED PRICE OR COST PLUS

In a fixed price subcontract, the supplier agrees to furnish specified items, materials, or services at a set price. This is the preferred arrangement from a quality point of view because the requirements are definite.

A "cost plus" subcontract provides that the supplier furnish items or services at his cost, plus a fee (or profit). This type of arrangement is used in the following situations:

- The item furnished cannot be easily defined—since perhaps it is still under development.
- The supplier has never made the item, and it is difficult to determine price.
- Design changes are expected as the work progresses.
- The buyer is not willing to wait until definitive requirements are available.

- Services are being procured, and they are on an as-required basis.

The cost plus contract has risks in that the supplier has less incentive to control costs, and requirements are not well-defined: the items furnished may not meet the customer's needs.

INTRA-COMPANY PURCHASES

Often one division of a company will manufacture a product that uses a part or component manufactured by another division of the same company. There may also be other suppliers who make a competitive item. Although there will always be exceptions, most manufacturers tend to treat the other division as just another supplier. Bids from the other divisions would be considered in competition with other suppliers, on a price, delivery, and quality basis.

Some companies have policies dictating the use of products produced in-house, whereas others allow free competition between internal and external sources. Past experience has shown that a restrictive policy does not work very well. When people know that they definitely have the order, they exhibit less concern for quality and schedule. The policy of competition between in-house and external suppliers seems to provide the best overall results. Frequently, however, company policies do dictate purchases within the company divisions.

QUALITY INFORMATION PACKAGE

Before a potential supplier can be evaluated effectively, it is necessary that the supplier be aware of the requirements expected. Part of any survey or evaluation will include questioning of the supplier, since it is necessary to assure that the supplier understands the quality standards and feels capable of meeting them. It is important to remember, however, that an evaluation is usually performed with a particular procurement in mind. The fact that a supplier produces good quality on certain products is not adequate evidence in itself that quality will exist in another product. Capability and familiarity with the particular product is essential.

At minimum, the following are required in the information package furnished to the potential suppliers:

1. Drawings and specifications
2. Descriptions of inspections and tests to be performed by supplier, including qualification tests
3. List of data and reports required from the supplier
4. Delivery schedule
5. Requirements for product identification, packaging, etc.
6. General conditions on the standard purchase order form to be part of the contract

The intent is to inform the vendor exactly what is needed.

EXISTING DATA SOURCES

Any given company has many suppliers, and any given supplier sells to many companies. Qualification and environmental tests are expensive and time-consuming. The cost of testing is especially high if several items are to be tested for each requirement, and if the item is destroyed in the testing process or no longer can be used as a salable product. If each company had to evaluate each supplier, there might be considerable duplication of effort, even though each company would be concerned with testing to its specific applications of the product. To some extent, then, it becomes economically feasible to pool data and share the results among users of the product. Sometimes a survey of the facility is carried out so that this information can be made available along with the test data. The data pool can take on any of a number of forms.

1. *Pooled information for a particular industry.* Companies in a similar industry often have similar needs and requirements. An example is CASE, for "Coordinating Aerospace Supplier Evaluation." Data on products is received by the organization and compiled by computer. The data can then be sorted by supplier, process, or product line. Member companies have agreed to furnish backup information upon request from other companies. Besides providing a cost saving to purchasing companies, CASE saves time in source selection. It is also advantageous to a supplier to have published data available on the supplier's products and capabilities.

2. *Government Programs.* The Government Industry Data Exchange Program (GIDEP) was developed to compile data on new parts and components. The primary objectives were economy and the availability of information to users.

3. *Company Programs.* Many large companies have programs for company-wide compilation of vendor data. This data can be the result of testing, surveys, or experience. The information is made available to all divisions in the company.

Any of these joint efforts can be of considerable value when a vendor is being considered or evaluated for ability to meet requirements. These types of efforts are usually worthwhile as long as the data are kept current and the system contains the test data for the specific environment indicated. Problems sometimes occur if there has been a design change to the item and the test data are not current. A supplier can usually tell prospective users where test data for the supplier's products are available.

QUALITY FACTORS TO
LOOK FOR IN A SUPPLIER

A supplier should exhibit an understanding of quality and its benefits, and should comprehend that an effective quality program provides benefits in terms of both inputs and outputs. On the output side we see better quality products with fewer defects discovered by the user. This can be translated into repeat sales and positive word-of-mouth comments, both of which result in greater sales. In terms of inputs, defective products at any stage of production call forth increased human resources, increases in materials used, greater use of energy, tied-up facilities, and attention by management. On the other hand, the by-products of high quality are better employee morale and reduced turnover of personnel.

Much can be learned about suppliers by the way quality is viewed within the supplier's organization.

- Does each manager see quality as part of his or her responsibilities?
- Do performance appraisals consider quality as an element of every manager's performance?
- Is the quality control department envisioned by company personnel when quality is mentioned, or does each person see quality as part of his or her own task?
- Are product problems covered up, or are they brought out in the open for resolution? Is there emphasis on blame for problems, or is the emphasis on cooperation to alleviate the problem?
- Is the company inspection-oriented or is the emphasis on prevention of defects?

• Do quality control personnel have the power to make decisions when there is an impact on product quality?

A company with a successful quality program should take a total approach to quality as part of its overall company strategy. This means that top managers place no less emphasis on quality than is placed on cost and schedule.

As Japanese companies open new plants in the United States, we notice close attention to selection of employees. These firms seek intelligent people who are reasonably well-educated with respect to their specific jobs. In addition, management seems more willing to delegate responsibility for quality of work to the worker and is willing to provide product use, cost, and other information to the employee as it relates to the particular job. Further, it seeks employees who have an attitude of cooperation and team spirit. The quality circles concept is based on these elements. Perhaps these are factors we should observe when evaluating a supplier.

PROBLEMS FOUND BY
SUPPLIER EVALUATIONS

In the evaluation of suppliers having quality problems, findings show a tendency for the different functions within the company to be working independently. One function—such as production planning, or marketing, or even quality control—proceeds with its own immediate objectives without consideration of other or overall needs, such as quality.

Some organizations view quality as either an unknown or an uncertainty. Rather than planning for quality, people wait to be told what to do. In some companies, an imbalance exists between product technology and production technology. New and stringent requirements appear in product designs without the equivalent advances in production technology. Manufacturing engineers are faced with the necessity of making tooling and equipment work at or beyond their tolerance capability. It is important to look at the supplier's total process and apply the proper controls to assure that the item is made right the first time.

In other problem companies, information flow is not synchronized with the flow of material. For example, drawing revisions are not released in time for use in procurement or manufacturing. This requires people to work with marked-up documents or under the threat of further changes. When the concept of quality is raised, the supplier people tend to focus on manufacturing defects. Companies with better quality records think of quality in broader terms. Companies with less satisfactory quality records often focus on acceptable quality levels, rather than on an attitude that any defect is unsatisfactory.

DOES THE SUPPLIER
USE ANY OF THESE?

Quality Control programs utilize various techniques. Since these techniques may be encountered in a supplier evaluation, some of the more well-known and frequently used ones are explained briefly. Complete chapters—or complete books in some cases—have been written on these topics. The objective here, however, is to provide an overview of each topic sufficient for a buyer to do his or her job. Checklist questions are also included, along with favored responses.

QUALITY PLANS

Some companies require that prospective or current suppliers prepare a plan defining exactly how quality is to be assured. Caterpillar Tractor Company, for example, provides a guideline for preparation of the plan by the supplier. The plan must identify control points throughout the supplier's operation, from receiving through shipping to the customer, including the following:

1. Major characteristics checked, and where in the operation they are checked
2. Frequency of checking
3. Method used in checking
4. Part of organization (i.e., QC, manufacturing, etc.) responsible for making the check
5. Records maintained, retention period, and traceability method

The plans are signed by supplier management people responsible for the operations and are submitted to Caterpillar management for approval.

QUALITY CIRCLES

Quality Circles are small groups of employees who meet on a scheduled basis. Their primary task is to identify problems, analyze them, and propose solutions. The concept began in Japan, and is directed largely toward quality problems—however, a wide variety of problems can affect quality. An important by-product of a quality circle is to improve communications between employees in different functional areas (such as engineering and manufacturing), and between employees and management.

Responses to the following questions will help the evaluation, or judge the effectiveness of the supplier's use of quality circles.

1. Is participation voluntary? (Yes—the success of quality circles is based on voluntary participation.)
2. Do circle members select their own problems? (Yes—one purpose of a quality circle is to identify *new* problems not yet recognized.)
3. With what frequency do they meet? (Weekly is typical.)
4. Are monetary awards given? (Preferably not—the most

effective circles are based on satisfaction gained in participating.)
5. How are problems handled when the circle identifies them? (Are documented results available?)
6. Are managerial people aware of results?
7. Do supervisors support quality circles?

DESIGN QUALITY INDEX

Manufacturing engineers and quality engineers often review designs to determine potential difficulties in manufacture or control of quality. At that time alternative designs can be rated with a design quality index (DQI) where one or more demerits are assigned to each difficulty. It is then more difficult to choose a design with an unfavorable index.

RELIABILITY OF DESIGN

Reliability is a measure of the product's ability to perform in the intended manner over the period of its expected useful life. Techniques are available for measuring the expected reliability of a design before the product is produced. This is helpful in selecting the better of alternate designs. It also is useful in identifying potential product problems so that changes are made in the design.

For any type of product, a supplier should be able to demonstrate a knowledge of reliability, how it applies to the product, and effort carried out to improve reliability in the product.

DESIGN REVIEW

When the engineering department has completed the drawings and specifications for a product, a design review is conducted. Engineering, quality control, production, procurement, tool design, and possibly other functions participate in the design review. The design is scrutinized, and its manufacturability assessed. Preliminary plans for tooling, routing, process controls, and inspection gauging are also established. Where solutions to problems are feasible, or improvements for producibility are apparent, changes can be made in the design before the final drawings are released.

The following are examples of questions that would be raised in the design review, which could alleviate later problems:

1. Can existing machines hold the tolerances specified?
2. Are unproven processes called for?
3. Is more than one supplier available for the purchased item or material?
4. Have life, reliability, and environmental qualification tests been performed?

The following are examples of steps that can be taken to control quality:

1. Design or procurement of inspection gauges
2. Design or procurement of test equipment
3. Preparation of process controls
4. Preparation of acceptance sampling plans
5. Initiation of life, reliability, or environmental tests to qualify product
6. Establishment of procedures for control of quality
7. Evaluation of suppliers

PRODUCTION SAMPLES—
FIRST PIECE INSPECTION

A determination of the adequacy of tooling made for a supplied item is best accomplished by checking items made with the tooling. Initial items are often made with model shop tooling, and it is important to check out the production tooling before the product goes into full production. It is important to check any other item if at any time there is a change in the tooling. In some cases the contractor will want the supplier to define the process controls used to ensure quality once production gets under way.

QUALITY AUDIT

Financial audits are commonly utilized by company managements and accounting firms to ascertain how closely accounting procedures and practices are being followed. A "quality audit" is similar in intent—it is performed to determine if a company adheres to procedures that can affect quality. Also, product conformance audits check a product prior to shipment, after normal acceptance tests and inspections are complete. It is not uncommon to find quality audits used to check all aspects of quality in a company. The objectives are to identify product inadequacies, nonconformances to procedures, or inadequacies in existing tests or inspections.

After supplier surveys are conducted, a quality audit of the supplier can be made. Any company, however, should also audit its own quality system. A supplier who shows evidence of auditing his or her own quality system can be expected to have a more mature quality control operation. Results of the supplier's own quality audits could be used as a basis for information needed by the survey team.

INSPECTION INSTRUCTIONS

While the blueprints or specifications define dimensions and other requirements, it is not always easy for the inspector or machinist to determine how to perform the inspection. Just as a manufacturing engineer may define how to make the item, the method of checking can be provided on an inspection instruction sheet. This defines the characteristics to be checked and the way it is to be done. It is especially important that the primary contractor and supplier personnel check for the same thing in the same way. Sometimes the inspection instruction will designate characteristics to be 100 percent inspected; in other cases a sampling procedure may be designated. In most instances, however, the number of items to check on a sample will depend on quality history for the particular dimensions or characteristics.

ZERO DEFECTS

The "zero defects" concept grew out of the defense and space programs, where there was great emphasis on high quality and reliability. The program recognized the involvement of personnel in quality improvement and aimed at prevention of defects. It symbolized the idea of doing the job right the first time. The program involves people at all levels of management and in all departments of a company. The objective is to motivate them to avoid mistakes. It places emphasis on pride in work, and on the unacceptability of defects of any nature.

Selection of a supplier with an active zero defects program can provide considerable assurance that there is an emphasis on quality at the supplier location. It does not, however, mean that further evaluation is unnecessary.

CLASSIFICATION OF
CHARACTERISTICS

A typical item purchased from a vendor may have a great number of requirements. For example, each screw may have a required diameter, length, thread size, head dimension, material, plating, etc. It becomes apparent that each characteristic of each item cannot be checked at incoming inspection. The objective of a classification of characteristics system is to provide guidance to inspection or test personnel as to the importance of the various characteristics. This does not imply in any way, however, that less important characteristics do not need to be met.

Some tolerances may affect safety, reliability, performance, or fit, whereas others may be specified by customary or standard tolerance priorities. It seems logical then that the frequency of checking could vary depending on the importance of a requirement. The controls built into a process would also affect the degree of checking required. Classification of characteristics is normally done during design and might appear on the drawing or other document. A supplier may also offer suggestions as to what characteristics are more important in an item.

It is imperative that everyone involved in subcontracting understand that when classification of characteristics is used, a low classification does not excuse nonconformance.

PARTS PER MILLION

Over past years many companies established an acceptable quality level (AQL) of 1 to 5 percent. This meant that the targeted defect level would be 1 to 5 percent in a lot of material. Recently, in recognizing that defect levels of that order of magnitude are completely unacceptable in international competition, many firms have specified defects in terms of parts per million. A figure of 100 PPM would be lower than a 1 percent AQL by a factor of one hundred. One of the main objectives is to be able to eliminate piece-by-piece inspections, or even sampling at incoming inspections. In evaluating a supplier, finding that PPM is used provides some assurance that the supplier is in tune with some of the latest quality control ideas.

VENDOR RATING SYSTEMS

Some contractors employ a vendor rating system which gives a quantitative rating to each supplier. The rating is usually based on results of past shipments, in terms of acceptance or rejection. The usefulness of a rating system depends on what goes into the rating figures and simplicity of use of the ratings. While a rating might be useful in highlighting better or worse vendors, it alone is insufficient to determine acceptability of a supplier.

Some vendor rating systems utilize only the results of acceptances or rejections at receiving inspections. They would then neglect latent defects found later in production or after the final product leaves the contractor's plant. Even if the system takes into account the seriousness of defects found, investigation is necessary to determine (1) which of the vendors' products has been rejected, (2) whether corrective action has been taken since, and (3) whether new products will introduce new problems. The general concept of a vendor rating system is to attempt to measure ability to control quality overall.

VENDOR SURVEYS

An evaluation or survey before a contract is signed does not assure that a vendor will comply with all requirements, but it will certainly help to indicate those vendors who cannot or will not comply. It would be more appropriate to say that a survey can help to ascertain those suppliers who *may* be able to comply. A survey cannot evaluate all aspects of a supplier's potential performance. The main purpose is to seek out the facts and to utilize them in making judgments as to the ability and desire of the supplier to fulfill the quality requirement. In some cases a problem or failure to perform results from a condition not evaluated in the survey. In other cases a problem derives from the purchasing company.

A survey team should examine the supplier's entire quality system by checking *where quality is controlled* throughout the supplier's plant, and *what control technique is used* at each point. Some methods are discussed in this chapter, while others related to inspection and testing are covered later. In addition, ascertaining the adequacy of equipment used to perform the check is very important.

PREPARATION FOR
A VENDOR SURVEY

Prior to preparing a vendor survey or visit to a supplier facility, the evaluators should undertake considerable preparation. First, it is necessary to become familiar with the drawings and specifications for the items to be procured. Knowledge of tolerances is important in order to evaluate the capabilities of the vendor's machines and equipment. Cleanliness requirements may make a special clean room necessary. Environmental requirements may require special testing chambers. Personnel with special assembly skills may also be important. A checklist is very helpful in determining what is to be observed in the survey, and as a way to record the findings. Often it is important that inspection equipment at the vendor's facility be compatible with the purchaser's equipment. In other cases the vendor may need certain equipment, since the purchaser does not have it.

OUTSIDE
EVALUATION SERVICES

Bringing quality control personnel to a supplier's plant can be expensive, especially when distances are great. If several companies are being evaluated as potential suppliers for one order, the costs can be prohibitive. One alternative is for a purchasing agent to contract with an outside professional service. The companies employ quality control professionals, who can handle quality control tasks. This is also an alternative for contractors who do not have their own professional staffs to perform surveys themselves.

COMPATIBILITY OF
MEASURING EQUIPMENT

Many quality problems result from nonagreement between test or inspection equipment at different locations. The differences can be in equipment calibration or precision, in the methods used when conducting the measurements, or in interpretations of standards. Differences between factory and field equipment often occur, as do differences between purchaser's and supplier's equipment. It is not uncommon for incoming inspection personnel to reject material, only to have the vendor say he has reinspected it, found it to be acceptable, and is returning it, only to have it rejected again. In the final analysis, it is not always the vendor who is found to be wrong.

As part of an initial supplier evaluation, any potential inconsistencies should be identified and corrected. Plans must be made for periodic correlation checks to avoid any variations from the original standards. Locating and correcting these deficiencies in compatibility may seem costly, but later losses in time and dollars can be much more costly.

CHECKLIST FOR VENDOR SURVEY

When conducting a quality survey of a supplier's or potential supplier's facility, it is easy to come into a situation where the supplier shows only what he wants to be seen. The good points would, of course, be emphasized by the supplier. A checklist provides a set of items that enable a company to evaluate on a consistent basis. It also provides a set of questions to which the supplier is asked to respond. The objective of the survey is to determine if the company being evaluated is doing the right things to achieve quality. It also attempts to determine if these things are being done in the right way.

The checklist includes a place to rate each of the items. The person or persons conducting the supplier survey should attempt to evaluate the supplier more from evidence as to what is done rather than from what the supplier may say is done. For example, the statement that design reviews are conducted must be verified. Written minutes of prior design reviews showing action items would be much better evidence. On the checklist in figure 3 many items to be rated also provide examples of evidence that can be requested. In some cases it may be possible for the evaluator to take a copy of the evidence back to the plant for further evaluation or future reference. The ratings are qualitative and it is necessary that the persons doing the survey be competent in the many quality control areas so that evaluations can be made as the item is discussed and evidence viewed.

The following can serve as guidelines in the use of the checklist ratings:

Outstanding: The supplier is judged to have a very effective system. (This rating would be rarely used.)

Good: The supplier's system appears to give very acceptable results.

Average: The methods and activities observed meet minimum standards in most cases, but some suggestions are appropriate.

Inadequate: Activities are not adequate to provide quality, or the function is not performed at all by the supplier.

FIG. 3-1

CHECKLIST FOR SUPPLIER SURVEY

QUALITY CONTROL POLICY	Outstanding	Satisfactory	Average	Inadequate
1. Is there a Quality Control Policy? (copies of policies or manual, copy of table of contents of manual)				
2. Are policies meaningful and appropriate? (Are responsibilities clearly defined in the manual?)				
3. Is there a procedures manual? Is the manual used? (Look for copies in use.)				

4. Does top management support quality? (Talk with top level managers; obtain views of quality control personnel.)

5. Do other department personnel respect the quality department?

6. Is the quality control budget adequate?

7. Are there reports of overall quality and quality costs? (Ask for copies of the reports; who sees and uses them?)

QC PERSONNEL AND ORGANIZATION	Outstanding	Satisfactory	Average	Inadequate
1. Are managers competent?				
2. Is the QC organization well defined? (Observe chart.)				
3. Where is QC placed in the overall organization? (Observe chart.) Who does QC manager report to?				
4. Adequacy of QC engineering personnel. (Talk to QC engineer.)				
5. Are QC supervisors on an adequate level?				

	Outstanding	Satisfactory	Average	Inadequate
6. Are inspection personnel competent? (Talk to them.)				
7. Obtain evidence of QC training. (Course outlines; talk to inspectors and others.)				
8. Are personnel motivated? Talk to a. Inspectors b. Shop personnel c. Shop supervisors				
SUPPLIER QC				
1. Do quality personnel review purchase orders before bids are obtained? (Talk to purchasing agent and engineer.)				

SUPPLIER QC	Outstanding	Satisfactory	Average	Inadequate
2. Do QC personnel participate in supplier selection?				
3. Is there a system for rating vendors? (Obtain a copy.)				
4. How are quality requirements communicated to vendors? (Obtain examples.)				
5. Is receiving inspection area adequate? (Visit area.)				
6. Are requirements specified to receiving inspection personnel?				

7. Are rejected lots properly identified and segregated?				
8. Are shipments awaiting inspection held in an enclosed area? (Inspect area.)				
9. Is purchasing notified of lot rejections?				
10. Are lots inspected before supplier is paid?				
11. Are quality characteristics identified for inspectors?				
12. Is sampling used and understood by the inspectors?				

QC IN MANUFACTURING	Outstanding	Satisfactory	Average	Inadequate
1. Are design reviews used?				
2. Do operators have means of checking their work? (Observe operators.)				
3. Is inspection adequate? (Are defects found later?)				
4. Are gauge calibrations current? Are calibration procedures adequate? Is a history maintained for each gauge?				

5. Are drawings available to operators and inspectors? Is there a system to assure changes are available?

6. Are defective items identified to prevent use? Are records maintained of defectives produced?

7. Are process control charts used?

8. Is there a system for quality improvement?

9. Is quality audit used? What actions are taken on problems found in the audit?

	Outstanding	Satisfactory	Average	Inadequate
FINISHED PRODUCTS				
1. Does QC participate in packing, storage, and shipping?				
2. Is there a system for handling customer complaints?				
FACILITIES				
1. Are QC facilities adequate?				
2. Is there a calibration lab?				
3. Are inspection areas clearly designated?				
4. Are test areas in good order?				

WORKING
RELATIONSHIPS WITH
SUPPLIERS

Of the three functional responsibilities of purchasing—that is, obtaining supplier items of the correct quality, at the right price, and on schedule—securing quality is the most demanding task. We have discussed the process of selecting the supplier and communicating the requirements to him. The next phase involves assuring that the products accepted are of the required quality. This phase can be divided into two steps: (1) motivating the supplier to produce and furnish the required quality, and (2) monitoring the supplier and his products. These functions depend to a large extent upon the establishment and maintenance of professional working relationships between the purchasing company and the supplier. This chapter will deal with motivation and working relationships. Verification of conformance to requirements will be covered in later chapters.

PAST PRACTICES
AND CURRENT GOALS

Historically, many purchasers relied on incoming inspection to verify the quality of items and material received. This was usually done at the purchaser's facility, but could also be done at the supplier's plant prior to shipment. Over the years the trend has been toward greater reliance on the supplier's quality system, and recently this trend has increased. The ultimate goal under this concept would be complete elimination of inspection upon receipt by the purchaser. The ability to utilize this concept successfully depends upon the purchaser establishing a very favorable working relationship with the supplier. In most cases buyers are reluctant to completely eliminate inspection upon receipt of the product—as a result, limited checking continues. Many Japanese and U.S. plants, however, have created a relationship with specific suppliers whereby there is essentially no incoming inspection.

RESPONSIBILITY FOR QUALITY

A workable supplier quality relationship places the responsibility for furnishing quality items on the supplier. Emphasis is on the supplier's use of a quality program that results in quality items being produced. The purchaser then requires evidence that this program continues in effect and that the items do meet the quality requirements. This evidence can be in the form of data showing results of tests and inspections performed by the supplier, backed by knowledge of the supplier's ability to control quality in the products. The purchaser may specify requirements for the supplier's quality system, but may also place inspection requirements in the subcontract.

QUALITY IS FIRM

The requirements in the purchase order must be considered firm, not as variables. Implications by the buyer in the dealings that something must be "good enough" will set up the wrong environment. The buyer and purchase order must be specific and firm so that everyone involved is absolutely clear on what is required. If the buyer does not take this firm approach, the supplier can hardly be expected to react in any other way. One way to clarify expectations is to return nonconforming material to the supplier and insist that only material meeting requirements be shipped.

Too often companies give the impression to their suppliers that compliance with requirements is not a serious business. Buyers apologize for the rejection of defective material, or depend on waivers or material review actions in order to avoid returning the material. When this type of approach is commonplace within a company, it is natural to expect the supplier to take advantage of the complacency.

What is the payoff for establishing a firm attitude in dealings with the supplier? The primary objective of a quality program is to have good material sent the first time. When a firm attitude is established, a company is more likely to receive usable items on time so that production schedules can be met. This contributes to productivity, as well as to the possibility of reducing or eliminating receiving inspection or testing. The Japanese have done this with the just-in-time inventory concept, where little or no receiving inspection is performed, and items arrive at the point of use in production as they are needed.

COST OF QUALITY

As stated by Harold A. Berry, "The cost of quality is never so high as when it is missing."[1] The buyer must be concerned with the total cost, and not just the price that will appear on the invoice for the orders. The total cost includes costs related to poor quality—such as costs of rejections, return of shipments, repairs, production delays, and costs related to customer receipt of products not fit for use. The buyer, however, must be cau-

1. Harold A. Berry, *Purchasing Guide*, (Englewood Cliffs: Prentice-Hall, 1964), Chap. 6.

tious not to pay more for goods that are actually not of better quality.

SUPPLIER QUALITY AUDITS

Audits for quality were discussed in Chapter 3. A company audits its suppliers on a periodic basis over the life of the subcontract. An audit is conducted in much the same way as the original survey, except that checks are for continuing compliance by the supplier. The checklist used during the survey could also be utilized in the audit.

CONTINUING COOPERATION

After the subcontract with a supplier is signed and in effect, there is a continuing need for good working relations between the contractor and supplier. This need applies through the stages of procurement as shown in figure 4-1. Each party must have certain information from the other that is essential to carry out the subcontract. Whenever information is exchanged affecting the contractual agreement, the new information should be made part of the contract. This is especially necessary for changes or clarification of requirements that are to be verified upon receipt of the goods.

Other information will be exchanged that does not result in a contract change. This includes items such as acceptance or qualification test data from the supplier or discussions related to problems arising in either facility. Sometimes problems will result in the need for corrective action by one of the parties. The resolution of problems is important to each party, and when problems occur it is not always easy to resolve them to both parties' satisfaction.

Since the vendor-supplied items are essential parts of the final product, any interruption to the vendor's delivery schedule

---

FIG. 4-1
STAGES IN PROCUREMENT
QUALITY CONTROL

---

1. Define and specify the quality requirements for the particular application.

2. Select suppliers who are ready, willing, and able to meet requirements.

3. Assure that there is a clear meeting of minds on the requirements.

4. Verify that goods received meet requirements.

5. Make disposition of nonconforming material and assure that corrective action is taken.

---

affects the overall production schedule. In a good supplier-contractor working relationship, it is expected that the vendor will advise the buyer well in advance if there are any expected or even possible delivery delays. For example, it is important that the supplier keep the contractor aware of a pending labor strike and progress in negotiations. Knowledge of quantities in inventory would also be helpful to the contractor in scheduling partial shipments. Favorable communications to the suppliers are helpful when schedules are met or quality is in conformance. Communications are not only for problems or criticisms.

Relations between the buyer and the supplier affect the smooth flow of communications and supplies between them, and the service is reduced when problems are encountered. Fast and effective service is often needed. Technical assistance before, during, and after the delivery is also important. It is necessary, however, to define the requirements for service and technical assistance as part of the agreement with the supplier.

SUCCESSFUL
SUPPLIER PROGRAMS

Many companies have presented their very own quality programs, each different in one way or another. Divisions within the same corporation often debate the merits of each approach. Certain features or characteristics tend to show up in the more successful programs.

1. Programs that are forced on a supplier are rarely successful.
2. Programs that tend to focus on one part of the organization have been shown to be less successful. Successful programs require top management support.
3. For successful programs, quality is a consideration in all activities from strategy formulation to performance evaluation of managerial personnel; all persons in the company should view quality as part of their job. As decisions are made, the impact on product quality should be considered. Successful quality programs show evidence of open cooperation between persons in the different functional parts of the organization.
4. The less successful programs tend to deal more with reaction than with action and more with placing the blame for problems than with preventing them.
5. Successful programs usually have quality professionals to design, implement, and measure results of the program.
6. Successful programs place emphasis on prevention of defects and on assistance to line operations.

7. Finally, companies with successful quality programs measure quality in terms of costs—and relate these costs to impact on net earnings and profits. Less successful programs deal with quality in terms of subjective statements such as "avoiding quality degradation." When a company places a dollar figure on quality (or lack of quality), it then finds it easier to invest funds in equipment, personnel, or research and development to attain that quality.

QUALITY RESPONSIBILITIES

There are many activities that must be carried out in order to attain a quality product. Some of these are normally performed by people in the quality control organization; others rightfully belong in other parts of the organization. For example, manufacturing personnel have the responsibility to make products meeting the standards and specifications. It would not make sense for someone other than the person making or working on the product to check each step of the work as it was performed. Thus, the worker must have a means of determining that his or her own work has been done properly. This may involve a measurement, or a means of controlling a process or machining operation, or verifying software, or all of these.

Similarly, the engineer is responsible for producing a design that will meet the needs of the user of the product. It is up to the engineer to ascertain these needs, by working with the customer's product definition, and then work with the manufacturing engineer to assure that the design can be manufactured with the equipment available to the people in manufacturing.

What then are the responsibilities of the purchasing department? The purchasing agent is fully responsible for administering the subcontracts and purchase orders; he must make sure that the supplier provides parts, materials, or services that conform to the standards given to him. The purchasing agent also has the responsibility to make sure that the supplier delivers material at the time scheduled. Defective parts are the same as no parts at all and can shut down production. Besides schedule and quality constraints, the purchasing agent has the further responsibility to negotiate a price favorable to the contractor. It might be said that the purchasing agent has the job of selecting the supplier with the lowest price from among the potential suppliers who can meet the quality and schedule requirements. In performing these duties, the purchasing agent utilizes the services of engineers, production schedulers, and quality control engineers. Each of them has a special know-how or skill that can be helpful in purchasing items meeting all of the requirements.

PURCHASING AND ENGINEERING

The engineer determines what is needed in the product design in order to meet the needs of the user. If the design contains parts or materials to be procured from a supplier, the requirements these parts or materials must meet are given in the design drawings and specifications. Although the engineer may suggest possible suppliers for a particular part or material, it is the responsibility of purchasing to assure that an appropriate supplier is selected. In some cases the buyer may need to insist that the engineer evaluate alternative suppliers' products. In this selection process the buyer may question requirements specified by the engineers if it is felt that any may be unnecessary, but the final decision must always be based on the engineering drawings.

The prices quoted by suppliers depend upon the severity of the requirements to be met. In the interest of the company, price is important, but is not to be reduced by sacrifice of standards unless the engineer determines that the particular requirement can be relaxed. If the engineer finds that a requirement can be changed, the appropriate drawing or specification must be changed. It is mandatory that the purchase order documentation, including the specification, exactly describe the requirements and that the buyer or anyone else obtain formal authorization of any changes. Specified requirements may be relaxed to reduce price, allow a standard item to be used, or permit the buyer to locate more bidders on the subcontract—but only if the needs of the product user are still met. In this process, anything unclear or ambiguous must also be corrected by the engineer. In general, an engineer who does his or her job well must consider the economics of obtaining or manufacturing the item and the advantages of having multiple sources, along with the necessary performance of the product.

PURCHASING AND PRODUCTION

The production department is responsible for determining the schedules for manufacturing. These schedules are provided to the purchasing department, where a procurement schedule is prepared. Purchasing needs an adequate lead time in order to evaluate and select suppliers for each part and material. This is especially true if some of the items have not been procured previously, necessitating qualification tests to assure that the items can meet the specified requirements. With an adequate lead time, a purchasing agent can do a better job of negotiating prices. Short lead times often result in special production runs, extra shipping costs, or missed delivery schedules, and can also result in failure to meet sales commitments, or even in shipment of products without completion of tests.

The lack of needed parts or raw materials can shut down processes or production lines. In a job shop, the results are less disastrous, but are still costly both in production delays and stoppages. In any case, frequent problems of this nature add to production costs and may result in loss of reorders or in dissatisfied users of the product. The purchasing agent is told by production what to buy, how much, and when it is needed. Even so, the purchasing agent also has the duty to question these factors, to be knowledgeable of latest products available, and to set sufficient lead times on orders. Perhaps an alternative material or a standard, less expensive item will suffice, especially if it is available now and the specified part is not. It is a responsibility of purchasing to be aware of new materials or parts as they become available and to question the design engineer and production scheduler as to their possible usage.

Sometimes an alternate part or material may cost more than the one specified or used in the past, yet the higher cost may be offset by lower in-house machining costs, longer life, or greater reliability. Both production and purchasing get involved in determining economic ordering quantities, since a large order may be received in partial shipments. There are storage costs, shipping costs, and inspection costs to consider in selecting the lot size for shipments. Purchasing becomes involved in trade-offs of these important but sometimes conflicting company objectives. With good departmental interrelationships, these conflicts can usually be resolved in the day-to-day operations.

PURCHASING AS A MANAGEMENT FUNCTION

Within the company, purchasing is a part of the functional organization just like marketing, finance, manufacturing, personnel, and other functions. In this sense, purchasing is a member of the management team, which works together to attain a profitable enterprise with a good company image for quality, price, and delivery.

QUALITY SYSTEM

Sometimes the term "quality system" is used to signify the collective group of activities, plans, and events that together are intended to assure that a product, material, process, or service will meet the standards and satisfy user needs. If customer satisfaction is not achieved, the system is not adequate. When we speak of purchased items, the needs of the contractor or the company ordering the purchased items must be satisfied. In addition, the needs of the ultimate user of the product also must be satisfied. Since the supplier is not always fully aware of the manner in which the product will eventually be used, it becomes the responsibility of the contractor to carefully define the requirements and standards the supplier's product must meet. The objective will be met if the standards are correctly established, management provides the proper quality emphasis, and the quality control program provides the assurance of compliance.

Returning to the concept of a quality system, the activities making up the system or program must be geared more to the avoidance of quality problems than to the resolution of problems after they occur. The system must be oriented toward making products correctly in the first place, rather than recognizing and sorting the good items from the bad. The purchasing agent has the responsibility of integrating the company's activities with those of the supplier to assure that the commodities meet all specified standards when they arrive on the receiving dock. Even if the defective items could be returned to the supplier for replacement at no cost, this course of action would not be satisfactory since the schedule may be adversely affected.

Products meeting the quality and reliability standards do not just happen. Achieving good quality through a successful quality system requires a commitment and investment by management. Management must provide the resources—especially people—to attain a successful system and keep it working without letup. The establishment of a top-notch quality system does not permit relaxation; it is merely the basis of an innovative and continuous process.

INFORMATION FLOW

Responsibility for supplier quality has been assigned to the purchasing agent in previous chapters of this book. Having this responsibility, it is important that the agent be aware of all communications with the supplier. It would not be acceptable for an engineer to advise a supplier that a product deviation is acceptable without securing a change in the purchase order requirement or processing a formal approval. In the absence of proper authorization, receiving inspection should reject the deviating lot upon receipt. Such problems can be prevented, however, if the responsible purchasing agent is aware of all communications. Therefore, most companies have established the policy of all formal communications with the supplier going through the purchasing agent.

We cannot say, however, that no one else should talk to the supplier. This is especially true if a resident engineer is maintained at the supplier's plant. It would be important for both companies to understand that these discussions may result in tentative agreement, which must be followed up by the purchasing agent's ratification.

We conclude that the best policy is for all information from suppliers to come into the company through the purchasing department. Likewise, all information going to the supplier should be sent by the purchasing department. This assures that the buyers are aware of all communications and that conflicting information is clarified before being transmitted.

Figure 4-2 shows most of the information that may be transmitted back and forth on a subcontract, although all of it does not apply to each subcontract. Some of the data is applicable to all subcontracts, while other information is required only if specified in the purchase order as a requirement.

SOME WIDELY USED CONCEPTS

For those dealing with suppliers and with other departments, an understanding of certain concepts is important. A few of these are described here and in other parts of this book.

FIG. 4-2.
FLOW OF PROCUREMENT INFORMATION
(CURRENT SUPPLIER)

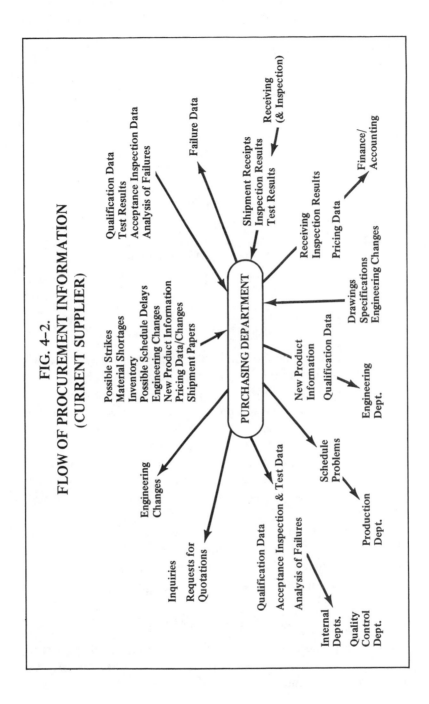

CONFIGURATION CONTROL

The term "configuration control" includes the control of design changes. In some cases, such as with newly developed products, it is not unusual to have many design changes. Since these changes can affect the form, fit, and function of the item with respect to the final product, it is important that a method be established to provide close control. It is easy to imagine the problems that might occur if goods received from vendors did not contain the design changes necessary to be compatible with the final product. The lack of a good drawing change control system is a frequent cause of friction between a contractor and the suppliers.

CORRECTIVE ACTION

It is essential to communicate with the vendor regarding any nonconformances found. A nonconformance may be found at receiving inspection, in the contractor's plant, or after shipment to the customer. Clarity and promptness are extremely important so that the supplier fully understands the problem as soon as possible. This may help prevent further manufacture of rejectable items by the supplier or further shipment of items with similar nonconformances. Often it is worthwhile for the supplier to come to the site where the nonconformance was identified or is occurring.

This will not only give the supplier a more precise view of the situation, but will also permit the supplier to see the extent of the problem it has caused. (Corrective action will be dealt with at greater length in Chapter 7.)

TRACEABILITY

Take a case where a product failure encountered during testing turns out to be the result of a supplied part. In order to solve the problems and obtain improvement in quality, it is necessary to first trace the items to the supplier. If there is more than one supplier of the part, this is a mandatory first step—however, it is not usually sufficient. It is further necessary to determine exactly when and where the quality problem originated. This means identifying the tools, people, dates, work shift, or material at the facility where the items were made. If tracing is possible we may be well on our way to preventing further occurrences. If we are unable to determine what went wrong and who was involved, corrective action becomes more difficult.

A system that provides traceability also has benefits in the prevention of defects. Our understanding of human behavior tells us that if a worker or inspector knows that defective work or overlooked defects in inspection can be traced back to him or her, errors might be avoided in the first place. Fear or pride in workmanship become operative when there is someone there to measure the quality and quantity of work done; traceability increases the incentive for quality.

SOME JAPANESE IDEAS

Japanese manufacturers employ a variety of techniques and concepts different from those most widely used in the United States. Some of these will be summarized relative to their impact on quality.

ORDER QUANTITIES

Textbooks deal with the EOQ (Economic Order Quality) concept, in which order costs are traded off against carrying costs to arrive at the optimum purchase order size. If sampling inspection were used to accept lots, its cost would be included as part of the order costs along with shipping costs. The buyer may also take advantage of blanket ordering and other techniques when selecting the order size. Smaller order quantities tend to place a greater burden on incoming inspection, since sampling inspection requires that proportionately greater samples be inspected as the lot size decreases.

CONSENSUS DECISION MAKING

The Japanese system provides for involvement by many in the decision-making process. The primary strength lies in the involvement of those responsible for the implementation of decisions reached. The system has certain drawbacks, including longer lead times necessary for reaching decisions and the problems related to rapid technological change. In U.S. companies, supplier related decisions usually involve participation of representatives from several company functions—so we do utilize consensus decision making to some extent.

JUST-IN-TIME (JIT) PURCHASING

The JIT concept as utilized by the Japanese involves ordering so that quantities arrive as required to meet manufacturing needs. Often the orders are delivered directly to the production line stations without incoming inspection. This eliminates inventory warehousing and associated storage losses, but places greater reliance on the supplier's quality control system. In some cases the purchase order will specify an overall quantity to be released in segments as part of a longer-term production schedule. In some cases manufacturing work centers are given order cards to release to the supplier as more items are needed.

EXACT SHIPMENT SIZE

In the United States it is common practice for suppliers to ship more or less than the quantity specified for a shipment. Because of this policy, it is necessary to count items upon receipt in order to verify the quantity for payment. Most Japanese companies specify and accept only the exact quantity. Items are usually packaged in boxes with compartments so that it is easy to verify the quantity. Parts are usually well packaged with no overages to allow for damaged parts or defective items. An exact quantity of all good items is expected by the buyer, and usually that is what is delivered.

ON-THE-JOB TRAINING

A Japanese employee continues in-company training until retirement as a regular part of the job. The employee is trained not only on things related to his or her own job, but in other jobs at the same level. This practice provides considerable flexibility in the work force and also helps develop people into generalists with a broader view of the company as a whole. In addition, it gives a person wider contacts within the company. We can expect that a purchasing agent with job experience in quality control might better perform his purchasing function. Likewise, a quality control engineer with purchasing experience would better perform the quality function.

SPECIFYING REQUIREMENTS

In the United States, design engineers tend to specify all requirements, including dimensions. The suppliers then must comply, or secure changes in requirements. The Japanese tend to simplify the specifications by relying more on performance requirements. This allows the supplier greater leeway for innovation in deciding how to meet the requirements. Critical dimensions would be given, allowing the supplier flexibility as long as performance requirements are achieved.

LIFETIME EMPLOYMENT

There are several other aspects of the Japanese management concept that have less direct applicability to a purchasing-quality control program. The Japanese policy of lifetime employment tends to provide increased loyalty to a company. At the same time, however, it gives the company less flexibility to handle changing product demands, changes in technology, and downturns in the economy.

REMUNERATION
BASED ON SENIORITY

The Japanese system depends largely on a seniority-based wage plan, where the pay is determined primarily by the number of years worked. Wage differentials almost entirely dependent upon age and length of service are prevalent in Japan. The idea is that this system eliminates the sometimes destructive competition between individuals and promotes a more harmonious working relationship. It also assumes that a person's responsibilities will increase as seniority increases, which becomes more difficult in periods of slow growth or business recession. It also is demoralizing to younger people when opportunities for promotion are not available.

WHEN PROBLEMS OCCUR

A typical scenario is set in motion when a quality problem occurs at the purchaser's facility. The supplier's component is assembled into the final product, but one-third of the finished units do not operate correctly. Negotiations with the supplier fail to correct the problem.

WHEN REJECTION OCCURS

Once it is determined that a supplier's material does not comply with the requirements, prompt action is important. It is necessary that the supplier be informed immediately, to prevent further production of defective items and to secure corrective action. It is further important to have the materials replaced with good items as soon as possible. The buyer's production and manufacturing people also need immediate warning, since there is likely to be an impact on their production scheduling. The design engineer should be informed, since it is necessary to determine the effect on performance of any products having the deficiency.

A supplier may react in different ways—but for now, let's assume that there is no disagreement that the item does not meet the requirement. Some possible supplier reactions, among others, are: (1) the items were satisfactory when shipped, (2) there is difficulty controlling the process, and (3) the shipment is within the AQL (Acceptable Quality Level).

When a supplier has continuing quality problems, one of the better approaches is to bring one or more of the supplier's people into the plant. Seeing a shut-down assembly line, piles of rejects, or other evidence often helps convince the supplier of the importance of the problem. It is best if the corrective action can be established while the supplier people are present, or soon thereafter. The scheduling of the corrective action should allow the buyer to follow up to assure that it is carried out. Elimination of the problem would, of course, be the final evidence of successful action.

Some people might think that it is better to send a task force to the supplier plant. This, however, places the travel cost burden on the purchaser. It also allows the supplier to control the meeting and show off more attributes than problems. It further tends to shift some responsibility for identifying the source of the problem to the purchaser. Probably most important, however, is that the supplier does not witness the actual defective items as they impact on the purchasing company. If the supplier really lacks technical know-how, however, a visit to the supplier's plant may be the better solution.

If there is a visit to the supplier, the buyer should certainly participate. The design engineer and quality control engineer are also essential. One thing the visitors should ask about is the supplier's corrective action process. Take a defective part and ask the supplier's people to go through the steps they take, starting from the time you, the buyer, advise them of a problem. Does the procedure result in assurance that the defect will not occur again? What if the supplier's corrective action procedure is inadequate? The buyer's team can make some suggestions, or show how their procedure works.

REVIEW OF
REJECTED MATERIAL

The Material Review Board (MRB) takes action when rejected material is urgently needed on the production floor and might be usable even though there is a nonconformity. It may be possible to repair the item and use it, or the defect may be such that performance is not affected. In any case, allowing use of the item after MRB approval is always contingent on defining the corrective action necessary to assure that the material with the defects will not be received from a supplier again.

It is certainly not appropriate to place rejected items before the MRB if the items are not urgently needed. MRB action may give the supplier a message that defectives may be all right after all.

The membership of the MRB varies, but would include the design engineer, quality control, and the manufacturing unit that will be using the item. It also makes sense to invite the buyer, even though he or she has no vote. Typically, rejection by any one member would mean the item is returned to the supplier.

Decisions for acceptance would include: (1) use as is, (2) use after specified rework, (3) sort the lot and use the good parts, or (4) combinations of the above. In each case, however, the acceptance can only take place if corrective action—which precludes receipt of further defective items—is obtained from the supplier.

ONGOING
PERFORMANCE EVALUATION

In our discussions we see that purchasing makes a significant contribution to the overall company, including contributions to product quality. Other areas in which purchasing has an impact are those of price and schedule. Although it may be more difficult to measure purchasing's achievement in quality, this does not negate the need for performance evaluation. A readily available measure is the number (or portion) of rejected shipments (or items) received. The compilation of rejects should include those found at incoming inspection, later in manufacturing, or even after the customer receives the end product.

MEASURE OF SUCCESS

We have discussed vendor rating systems to evaluate suppliers, but the real source of success for a supplier quality program is the buyer. With a vendor rating system, the buyers choose from among the vendors rated as satisfactory. A buyer rating system places further incentive on the buyer to go beyond simply selecting the highest-rated vendor. The buyer could go further to improve his or her own performance by obtaining continuing quality improvement.

One way to rate buyers is to measure the cost of poor quality. This cost would include the expense of rejections, rework, servicing, inspection and test of replaced goods, design changes related to defective work, or delayed schedules due to lack of supplied items. The cost could be measured as a percentage of payments to the suppliers.

LEGAL
ASPECTS

The legal aspects of contracts and purchasing are extensive. It is the objective in this chapter to discuss those aspects of the law that relate to quality of purchased material. Although most purchasing agents and buyers are familiar with these legal factors, quality control people and design engineers are less likely to have acquired this knowledge. Since these people become involved in subcontracts, it is important that they have some understanding of the laws. This background may be useful in requirements preparation, in dealings with suppliers, and in matters involving inspection, acceptance and compliance of purchased commodities, services, or data.

Buyers and sellers are covered in their dealings by the Uniform Commercial Code (UCC). This code was prepared to provide consistency in buyer-seller relations and to remove some of the risks that previously existed due to uncertainties as to how the law would decide a particular contractual disagreement.

AUTHORITY AND AGENCY

The purchasing agent and buyer are legally considered agents for their company in that they are delegated the authority to act for the firm. They deal with salespersons who are considered agents of the supplier. As an agent of the company, a buyer is delegated the authority to act for the company in dealings with suppliers. Other persons, such as design engineers or quality control people, deal with their supplier counterparts, but are not usually authorized to make binding agreements. The activities of the purchasing agent or buyer—who serves as the official representative or agent for the company in dealings with suppliers—fall under the *law of agency*. In simple words, an agent is someone who has been given the power to act for another person or organization, called the principal. An agency agreement will always specify the degree of authority that is delegated to the agent. This agreement, however, can either be expressed or implied.

The purchasing agent then has the authority to bind the company (principal) to subcontracts. Most companies, however, closely define to buyers just what they are authorized to do, and situations in which higher approval is necessary.

It is important for each person dealing with supplier personnel to recognize the scope of his or her own individual authority, and to make it known to the supplier people involved. In this way, legally enforceable agreements will be created only by those so authorized. An unauthorized person who implies that he or she has the authority to make agreements, may bind the company by actions or statements.

CONTRACTS

A contract between the purchaser and the supplier contains the requirements for the goods and/or services to be supplied. The contract can be in the form of a purchase order or a more detailed document, depending on the degree of definition needed. Generally, more complex items require more description in the contract.

ELEMENTS OF A CONTRACT

Certain basic elements must be present before a valid contract exists. There must be two or more parties to the contract. Also required is an offer by one party and acceptance by the other. The offer must identify—as a minimum—the price, quantity, subject matter, and parties. The acceptance must conform to all terms of the offer; any additional terms are considered a rejection of the original offer and the communication of a new offer. For example, a supplier offers to supply one hundred units that meet a given specification, for $50,000, and the purchaser accepts the offer. The supplier would then be obligated to supply the items in accordance with the specification, and the purchaser would be obligated to pay the agreed amount. As another example, the promise by S to furnish a test set is not a contract until accepted by B. Furthermore, it must state the consideration to be given by B, in the form of money, an act, or agreement to forebear action (such as agreement by B not to return a prior shipment of nonconforming items received from S.)

In the typical contract each party acknowledges agreement to the terms. Written agreements are preferred, but oral contracts are valid within legal definitions. A contract can be created by an offer by one party and an act by the other. For example, buyer Y offers to buy ten items, catalog No. 601, from supplier X. Supplier X receives the offer and ships the items. The act by X created an implied acceptance—a contract then came into existence.

Take another example where quality control and purchasing are both clearly involved. A purchase order agreement specifies fifty items at $100 each. Upon receipt, purchaser's receiving inspection discovers a nonconformance. The supplier then offers to reduce the price to $75 each if purchaser will keep half the shipment. The return of half the shipment to supplier would be an act of implied acceptance of the offer.

Assume a supplier publishes a catalog listing an item at $50 each. Buyer *B* responds with an order for ten items. Does a contract exist? Probably not. A catalog is usually considered a declaration of intent to receive offers. The supplier must accept each specific order before a contract exists.

ORAL CONTRACTS

If an oral contract can be proved, it is valid. Frequently, however, it is not easy to prove. Witnesses are one means of proving an oral agreement. Even if an oral contract can be proved, however, it will not stand up if (1) there is a written agreement with conflicting terms, or (2) it falls into a category of contracts that the laws of the particular state specify must be in writing. Most state laws and the Uniform Commercial Code state that contracts involving $500 or more must be in writing to be enforceable. It is the best policy, of course, for a buyer and seller to make all agreements in writing to lessen the likelihood of later disagreements. There are certain legal requirements for creation of valid written contracts—such as an offer, an acceptance, and signatures of the parties. There is, however, some variability in the exact procedures.

Assume that a buyer and supplier representative reach a verbal agreement. The UCC provides that when a seller sends a written confirmation of his or her understanding of the verbal agreement, the buyer has ten days to give written notice of any objections. If no objections are given, both parties are bound to a contract. If the buyer responds with objections within the ten-day period, neither party is bound. In the latter case, either party could then make a new offer and attempt to obtain agreement.

DIFFERING TERMS

If a purchaser supplies a specification or a written offer to purchase, these can be accepted or rejected by the supplier. Assume the supplier submits alternative terms, or sends an acknowledgment of the order containing differing terms. By common law this is considered a counteroffer, and the original offer is terminated. It is then the buyer's turn to accept or reject the counteroffer. This acceptance can be express, or it may be implied by acceptance of the goods from the supplier.

The provision in the Uniform Commercial Code differs from this common-law concept. In the initial dealings, possibly following verbal discussion or agreement, the buyer may follow up with a purchase order to the supplier. Assume again that the purchase order specifies requirements and conditions. Then the supplier sends an acknowledgment accepting the order, but does so on the supplier's own form which contains different terms. The UCC provides that the terms expressed on the acknowledgment become additional terms of the subcontract, unless (1) the original purchase order specifically objected in advance to any further terms, (2) the new terms make substantial difference in the goods with respect to their usability, or (3) the buyer objects to the terms within a reasonable time.

A court upheld a subcontract clause on the acknowledgment, which stated that no warranties were provided, even though the original purchase order specified that a warranty was to be provided as part of the order. The UCC operates to the advantage of the buyer in cases of differing terms, and the buyer can further protect the company by taking the following precautions with respect to the purchase order:

1. The order should expressly limit acceptance to "the terms herein. Any additional or different terms proposed by the seller are hereby rejected."
2. In each original purchase order, object to all "other terms" in advance. Use a clause such as "The only contractual terms with the supplier are those found in this purchase order."
3. Examine acknowledgments and other forms closely.

Promptly object to any unacceptable clauses. If the supplier ships the goods without recognition of the objection, don't accept or use the goods until the objection is resolved.

FIRM OFFERS

Upon receipt of an offer by a supplier to furnish goods at a specific price, the buyer may need to delay acceptance in order to check other vendors for price, and also check within the company for technical acceptability of the goods offered. The UCC provides that when a supplier makes a written offer in response to a request for bid (or request for quotation), and also sets a time the offer will be held open, the offer cannot be retracted before the specified date. If no time limit is specified, the offer remains open for a reasonable time (but not over three months). This provision of the UCC gives the buyer assurance that he or she can evaluate the bids received and award the subcontract without the risk that the offer may be withdrawn in the meantime.

HONEST MISTAKES

Mistakes can occur in the preparation of a purchase agreement, specification, or bid. Considerable care should be exercised to avoid errors, since they are not always easily corrected. If there were an error and the dispute could not be settled without litigation, the conditions of the particular case would determine its outcome. It can be generally said that a mistake by only one party to the contract does not make the contract void unless the other party is aware of the mistake or should have been aware of it. As an illustration, consider the following examples:

A vendor intends to quote a price of $950 but through a typing error instead quotes $910, which is transmitted to the purchaser. If the buyer accepts the offer without knowledge of the error, a court will probably hold that a valid contract exists.

If, in the above case, the price was typed in error as $95, a court would probably hold that the buyer should have recognized the error, and therefore the contract is void.

Minor mutual mistakes in the contract do not affect its validity. Factual errors that materially affect the agreement, however, would render the agreement void. For example, buyer B agrees in the contract to purchase the remaining five units of Model X test equipment at a reduced price. Unknown to the buyer and seller, the units were severely damaged by fire yesterday. The contract would be void.

A buyer or seller should not assume that an error will result in a void contract. Therefore, extreme care must be taken in preparation of the document.

REASONABLE TIME

Schedules or dates for a vendor's or supplier's action are usually specified in the purchase order. Courts seldom set aside time requirements as being unreasonable if both parties have agreed to them. Where a time is not specified in the contract, the UCC and courts will decide whether the action took place in a "reasonable time."

The time allowed for acceptance or rejection of material by a purchaser is often a subject of controversy. Another area of controversy can be the time allowed for acceptance of an offer made by a vendor. A buyer who waited seven months, and then wrote accepting a vendor's offer was said by a court to have waited too long. It was not a reasonable length of time.

In another case, five months was found not to be an unreasonable period of time to reject defective goods. In this case the buyer had identified a problem with the goods when received, but the supplier had given assurance that the problem would be taken care of and sent a representative to observe the defects. The defects were never corrected by the supplier. Under these circumstances the court held that five months was not an unreasonable period of time for rejection.

Precedence can be established by actions under prior situations. If in the past a supplier had taken back goods after the purchaser had them for forty-five days, this could establish forty-five days as a reasonable time even if the contract specified thirty days for acceptance. Usual and customary practices in the particular trade also work to establish reasonable times. In each case, however, a court will observe any factors that may cause the case at hand to be unique.

SHIPMENT AND RECEIPT

AUTHORIZATION TO SHIP

Often a contract will specify a method of packing and shipment. If there is no provision in the contract, the purchaser, according to the Uniform Commercial Code, may designate the method. The law, however, expects the buyer and the seller to cooperate toward meeting the overall objective of the purchase order. What if the seller notified the buyer that goods were ready for shipment and requested instructions and/or authorization? The purchaser is required to provide these instructions—failure to do so can be considered a breach of the contract by the purchaser. In general, a court will expect both parties to cooperate.

In cases where the supplier has goods ready for shipment, but the buyer has the responsibility to furnish instructions and does not do so within a reasonable time, the seller can do any of the following:

1. Proceed to ship by a reasonable method
2. Sell the goods to a third party, and claim damages from

the buyer if the price obtained is less than the contract
price
3. Claim breach of agreement and cancel the purchase
order
4. Expect to have a valid reason for delay in shipment

In its decision, a court will consider whether each party is attempting to cooperate to achieve the requirements of the purchase order.

GOODS IN SEPARATE LOTS

The UCC defines an installment contract as one that specifies or
permits delivery of the goods in separate lots to be accepted or
rejected separately. Many subcontracts involve the shipment of
goods in separate shipments or lots. Receiving inspectors, quality control personnel, the design engineer and production schedulers, along with the buyer, can become involved in accep-
tance/rejection decisions involving individual lots. Therefore, legal
implications are interesting and often significant to each of these
persons.

A contract can specify schedules for deliveries in lots. However, deliveries in installments can also arise by specific agreement between parties or based on certain circumstances—such
as the supplier having insufficient items available. Any specific
installment may be rejected by the purchaser for nonconformities. The buyer also has other options as discussed elsewhere that
apply to any shipment. Sometimes a purchaser will allege that
nonconformance of a lot or installment affects the value of the
entire contract and that therefore a contract breach has occurred.
The provisions of the UCC are based on the concept that the
contract should be preserved as long as an undue burden is not
placed on either of the partners. Beyond that, if the buyer and
seller cannot reach an agreement, a specific case will have to be
settled in court.

The court will consider all aspects of a case. In one instance a contract provided for deliveries of two hundred units per month for twelve months. Some shipments were as much as three weeks late, and two shipments were rejected for nonconformities. The purchaser wrote, canceling the subcontract, and the supplier filed a countersuit for damages, citing changes in design requirements as a cause of the delays. In finding for the supplier, the court pointed out that (1) there was no evidence of the buyer showing earlier concern as the delayed shipments were received, (2) the supplier had replaced all rejected items, and (3) there were changes in requirements subsequent to the original schedule. In any case, courts will look unfavorably on purchasers who do not cooperate toward resolving problems related to defects. The supplier, however, remains responsible for costs related to defective or nonconforming products.

A buyer can lose the right, by law, to claim a breach in the overall contract for a particular nonconformity if he or she accepts any lots with that nonconformity without notifying supplier of intent to claim a contract breach.

SPECIAL TOOLING

In many subcontracts, the purchase order requires that special production or inspection tooling be made for the order. The terms of the purchase order will govern the ownership of the tooling and the date payment is due. Unless specified otherwise, the supplier can expect payment and bill the buyer when the tooling is completed and proven (or inspected). It is not necessary that the tooling be received at the purchaser's facility.

DELAY IN PERFORMANCE

Delays can occur in delivery, service, inspection, test, or other task identified by date in the purchase order. If any requirements are not met by the specified date, the UCC considers it a breach of contract, except where compliance in good faith with a government order or directive—domestic or foreign—caused the delay, or an event occurs beyond the control of the supplier which the buyer and seller assumed would not occur. In either case, if the supplier has some items, but not enough to meet outstanding orders, the available items must be allocated among all contracts.

When a buyer receives notification from a supplier that delivery will be delayed indefinitely, the buyer is allowed to terminate any unfulfilled portions of the agreement. The term "cover" is defined as a buyer's discretionary right to buy goods elsewhere when the seller wrongfully fails to deliver the goods as required under the contract (UCC 2-712). What if the buyer is insecure and anticipates a breach in contract? The buyer has the right to demand written assurance from the seller.

TITLE TO GOODS

When the purchasing company takes title to goods, the purchaser assumes responsibility for risks or damages that may subsequently occur to the goods. If the goods are shipped F.O.B. the seller's facility, the purchaser takes title at the time the carrier takes the goods. The seller is, however, obligated to follow buyer's instructions in the contract as to packaging and shipping, or to utilize reasonable packaging and packing methods.

RISK OF LOSS

The UCC provides that when not otherwise agreed, the risk of loss passes to the buyer on receipt of the goods. This places the responsibility for shipping damage, theft, or destruction upon the seller or the transporting agent up until the time of receipt.

What if the customer requested the seller to hold the goods past the date of intended shipment? In a recent case the supplier allowed the customer to leave purchased goods on the supplier's property for a few days. During those few days the goods were severely damaged and the purchaser refused to take them, claiming that the vendor was responsible. The court held that since the parties did not have any agreement on the risk of loss, and the vendor could have required the buyer to accept the risk before allowing a delay in pickup of the goods, the vendor had the risk of loss according to provisions in the UCC.

INSPECTION AND
ACCEPTANCE OF GOODS

The terms of the contract concerning inspection and acceptance govern the place, time and/or method of inspection. In any case, the buyer is entitled to inspect all goods to determine conformance to requirements. However, this right cannot accrue until the goods are identified with the contract, or are tendered or delivered. "Nonconforming goods" are those not in accordance with any obligation under a contract (UCC 2-106[2]). The law gives the buyer the right to perform this inspection before payment is made, unless there is an agreement to the contrary.

The costs of performing the inspection are the responsibility of the purchaser, unless the contract specifies otherwise or the inspection reveals that items do not conform to the requirements. Also, the buyer is entitled to recover costs related to return of the nonconforming items plus damages suffered—such as those resulting from his customers' cancellation of orders.

ACCEPTANCE OR REJECTION

If the goods do not conform to any requirements, the purchaser has certain options as follows:

1. Reject the entire lot or shipment
2. Accept a portion of the shipment and reject part (How-

ever, normal commercial units, such as drums of oil, cannot be divided without seller's permission)
3. Accept the shipment as is, or accept it subject to a reduction in price

The purchaser has certain obligations when material is rejected. Failure to fulfill these obligations may result in the purchaser's loss of the right to return the material.

1. The seller must be notified of the rejection promptly or within a reasonable time of the discovery of the nonconformity. The term "cure" refers to the right of the seller to remedy nonconforming goods shipped to the buyer prior to the date final performance of the contract is to take place (UCC 2-508).
2. The buyer must specify what the nonconformity is and how it was determined.
3. The buyer must request instructions for disposition of the goods from supplier, holding goods for a reasonable time.
4. The buyer must carry out any instructions given by the supplier regarding disposition of the nonconforming material.

A purchaser has a reasonable period of time to accept shipments, or the materials may be presumed to be accepted. If a shipment is accepted, the buyer becomes obligated to pay, and the ability to later reject is waived where the reasons for rejection could have been observed by a reasonable inspection. Defects later discovered are valid reasons for revoking the acceptance if the defects could not have been easily determined upon receipt. In any case, the purchaser is obligated to notify the supplier promptly whenever the nonconformities are discovered. If, however, the buyer indicates rejection but goes ahead and uses materials in question, acceptance is deemed to have occurred.

On the other hand, if the seller induced the purchaser to accept a shipment without inspection by assurances that the material conformed, the purchaser may retain rights to reject later.

In some instances a supplier will send parts or materials on approval or on some other basis, stating that the receiver has a reasonable time to try them and/or decide whether to keep them. In this case, the receiver has a reasonable amount of time to decide upon acceptance or return. The buyer has this option whether or not the goods conform.

BUYERS' RIGHTS—EXAMPLE

In one case a unit arrived from the supplier but failed to meet the specifications in the contract. Upon notification of the problem, the supplier attempted to correct it. The purchaser had placed a deposit on the unit, but agreed that if the deposit were returned, no other action against the supplier would be taken. The supplier, however, refused to return the deposit. The purchaser found another unit which he purchased from a different supplier at a higher price, and filed suit against the seller to recover the deposit plus the price differential.

The court awarded the buyer the deposit return plus the price difference, saying that the buyer's offer to settle for return of the deposit was based on immediate return of the deposit. There was no question as to a purchaser's right to seek replacements when goods do not conform to the contract requirements.

REVOKING ACCEPTANCE

The buyer has the right to revoke a prior acceptance if (1) the buyer's acceptance of nonconforming goods was based on a reasonable inspection, which did not reveal the defects, or (2) the buyer accepted nonconforming goods under the reasonable assumption that the nonconformity would be corrected, and it was not corrected within a reasonable time. A revocation of an acceptance must occur within a reasonable time after discovery of the nonconformity, and cannot occur after the goods have been substantially changed in condition from causes other than the original defect.

INSPECTION CLAUSES—
COMPLEX EQUIPMENT

Standard inspection clauses usually appear in purchase orders for morc complex equipment. The following clauses are typical:

1. *All supplies shall be subject to inspection and test by the purchaser to the extent practicable at all times and places including the period of manufacture, and in any event prior to acceptance.*

2. *In case any supplies or lots of supplies are defective in material or workmanship or otherwise not in conformity with the requirements of this contract, the purchaser shall have the right either to reject them (with or without instructions as to their disposition) or to require their correction. Supplies or lots of supplies that have been rejected or required to be corrected shall be removed or, if permitted or required by the purchaser, corrected in place by and at the expense of the supplier promptly after notice, and shall not thereafter be tendered for acceptance unless the former rejection or requirement of correction is disclosed. If the supplier fails to promptly remove such supplies or to replace or correct such supplies, the purchaser either (i) may replace or correct such supplies and charge to the supplier the cost occasioned; or (ii) may terminate the contract for default as provided in the clause of this contract entitled "Default." Unless the supplier corrects or replaces such supplies within the time specified in the delivery schedule, the purchaser may take*

the delivery of such supplies at a reduction in price that is equitable under the circumstances.

3. If any inspection or test is made by the purchaser on the premises of the supplier, the supplier without additional charge shall provide all reasonable facilities and assistance for the safety and convenience of the purchaser's inspectors in the performance of their duties. All inspections and tests by the purchaser shall be performed in such a manner as not to unduly delay the work. The purchaser reserves the right to charge to the supplier any additional cost of purchaser's inspection and test when supplies are not ready at the time such inspection and test is requested by the supplier or when reinspection or retest is necessitated by prior rejection.

4. Acceptance or rejection of the supplies shall be made as promptly as practicable after delivery, except as otherwise provided in this contract; but failure to inspect and accept or reject supplies shall neither relieve the supplier from responsibility for such supplies that are not in accordance with the contract requirements nor impose liability on the purchaser therefor. The inspection and test by the purchaser of any supplies or lots thereof does not relieve the supplier from any responsibility regarding defects or other failures to meet the contract requirements that may be discovered prior to acceptance. Except as otherwise provided in this contract, acceptance shall be conclusive except as regards latent defects, fraud, or such gross mistakes as amount to fraud.

5. The supplier shall provide and maintain an inspection system acceptable to the purchaser covering the supplies hereunder. Records of all inspection work by the supplier shall be kept complete and available to the purchaser during the performance of this contract and for such longer period as may be specified elsewhere in this contract.

ARBITRATION

Where problems involving contract disputes between buyer or subcontractor cannot be resolved, either party can bring suit. Some contracts call for arbitration by a third party to settle the dispute, or both parties may agree to arbitration rather than have the disagreement go to litigation. When there is such an agreement, the arbitration becomes binding.

FRAUD

It is important to briefly review the definition of fraud as it may impact on quality. Any misrepresentation of the quality or performance of supplied goods can be considered fraud if all of the following are true:

1. The statement was made before the contract agreement was signed.
2. The statement was untrue and the seller knew it to be untrue, or it was recklessly made.
3. The statement was made for the purpose of inducing the other party to act on it.
4. The other party did, in fact, rely on the misrepresentation.
5. The other party was damaged by the reliance.

Thus we can see that (1) a false statement after the subcontract was signed is not fraud. (2) If the seller was expressing an opinion on quality, it would not constitute fraud. (3) If the buyer or the buyer's representative has previously inspected the goods, the purchaser may have assumed responsibility. The latter is true, however, only if the purchaser has the skill and ability to ascertain that a particular defect existed. Generally the purchaser has a right to reject materials at a later date for previously undiscovered defects.

WARRANTIES

Quality exists if material conforms to the requirements at a point of acceptance. Reliability exists if this conformance continues for a specified period of time. A "warranty" is a guarantee or assurance by the seller to the purchaser that the goods are or shall be as represented. The Uniform Commercial Code defines "warranty" as any affirmation of fact, express or implied, by a seller of goods to the buyer as part of a contract of sale (UCC 2-312 to 2-315). A warranty usually specifies that the product will continue to meet some or all of the requirements for a specified period of time. It also defines the actions to be taken if the product fails to perform as promised.

EXPRESS OR
IMPLIED WARRANTIES

Warranties can be either express or implied. Express warranties can be stated in contracts, purchase orders, advertisements, or catalogs. They can be written or oral, but written warranties are preferred since there is less room for disagreement on the intention. Although it is better to have warranty agreements formally stated in the contract, statements in letters or other communications are sufficient. In a recent case, a supplier's oral warranty was recorded on tape. The court said it was valid even though it exceeded the standard written warranty made by the supplier. Usually, however, for a warranty to be valid, a company must have done one of the following: (1) notified the buyer of the salesperson's authorization to make the guarantee, (2) confirmed the guarantee, or (3) maintained a tradition of accepting responsibility for salespersons' guarantees in past dealings. Courts have recognized that salespersons tend to "puff" their products, so care is required in separating "puffing" from a guarantee.

Whether there is a written warranty or not, there is an *implied warranty* by a supplier that the goods or services are fit for the ordinary purposes for which they are intended. In addition, if the buyer makes known to the seller the specific use for which the goods are intended, and relies on the seller's knowledge and judgment, there is an implied warranty that the goods will be reasonably fit for that specific purpose. If an express warranty conflicts with the implied terms, the express warranty governs. Implied warranties are covered as part of the Uniform Commercial Code (2-312 to 2-315) as shown in figure 5-1.

In order to take maximum advantage of the implied warranty of fitness for use, it is suggested that a buyer make technical information on use available to the supplier, seek the supplier's advice on specifications, and have the supplier's representatives meet with users for discussion of usage.

TIME IS A FACTOR

Although a warranty may extend for a period of time, the purchaser has the obligation to make a claim to the supplier as soon as product or service deficiencies are recognized. Courts have thrown out cases in which the purchaser took an unreasonable amount of time to determine that a condition of deficiency existed. If a deficiency could be easily observed at receiving inspection, a later claim may be invalid. This is especially true if the supplier specifies a limit on the time—such as 30 days—during which a claim can be made.

Many deficiencies, however, cannot be ascertained until the items have been assembled into larger units, or are later tested or placed in actual use. Many warranties state that the goods will continue to work as intended for a specified period of time after being placed in use.

DENIAL OF IMPLIED WARRANTY

A supplier may deny an implied warranty of merchantability or fitness for use, but this must be done in a conspicuous manner.

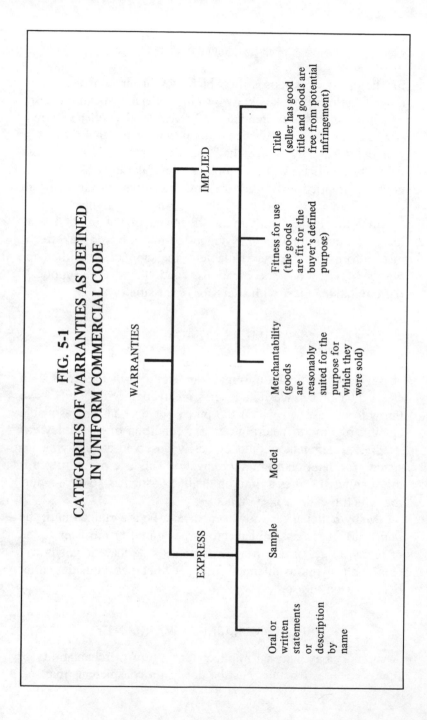

FIG. 5-1
CATEGORIES OF WARRANTIES AS DEFINED
IN UNIFORM COMMERCIAL CODE

WARRANTIES

EXPRESS

IMPLIED

Oral or written statements or description by name

Sample

Model

Merchantability (goods are reasonably suited for the purpose for which they were sold)

Fitness for use (the goods are fit for the buyer's defined purpose)

Title (seller has good title and goods are free from potential infringement)

Disclaimers in small print on the back of documents or on the printed forms are not considered sufficient. If it is the seller's intent to disclaim a warranty of merchantability or fitness for use, the contract must use those words or other language clearly stating that there are no implied warranties. A disclaimer must be in print larger than the rest of the document, in a different color, or in contrasting type, to catch the buyer's eye.

In a recent decision, a Pennsylvania Supreme Court ruling indicated that a supplier must be very specific in contract language if it is desired to disclaim a warranty. The court ruled that an implied warranty of merchantability under UCC 2-316 cannot be excluded unless the term "merchantability" is used. Also, an implied warranty of fitness for a particular use can only be excluded if the contract states that no warranties exist beyond the face of the agreement. Terms such as "as is" or "with all faults" are typical statements of disclaimer, but they must be conspicuous in order to be valid.

UCC AND WARRANTIES

The Uniform Commercial Code deals at length with warranties and promises by the supplier and the purchaser. In general, the UCC provides for greater faith of the buyer in statements provided by the supplier. The terms provide that an express warranty is created as follows:

1. Promises made by the supplier to the buyer are valid and shall be complied with.
2. Descriptions of the materials furnished are a warranty that the goods will conform to these descriptions.
3. Samples of the goods supplied during the bargaining process imply that the goods supplied are to conform to the sample.

The legal complexities of the UCC present some difficulties to the buyer, design engineer, and quality control engineer. They are summed up by John D. Jackson as follows: [1]

1. Where an offer is made in writing by a seller, he or she must live up to it for the time specified.
2. Verbal agreements are binding, but it is best to confirm them in writing.
3. Terms stated in the specifications and purchase order which conflict with seller's disclaimers or terms in acknowledgments, are usually resolved in the buyer's favor.
4. A buyer can expect items furnished to be fit for the use described to the seller.

The UCC also provides for cases when a disclaimer is inconsistent with an express warranty in the contract. The UCC states clearly that the warranty governs if there is any inconsistency.

These provisions in the UCC provide greater peace of mind in that the buyer can depend on express or implied warranties without having to worry about trick phrases or small print in unusual places.

1. John D. Jackson, "Uniform Commercial Code: It's a Bonus for Buyers," *Purchasing Magazine* (Feb. 6, 1969):54.

EVIDENCE OF
CONFORMANCE

Companies procuring goods from suppliers have the task of determining whether the goods conform to the requirements of the purchase order. This is true even if much of the responsibility for quality is delegated to the supplier. The importance of specifying requirements clearly and accurately has been established in earlier chapters. Both the supplier and the buyer should be in agreement as to exactly what is to be furnished.

The purchasing company must then determine how conformance is to be judged to assure that the goods conform to the requirements. In some cases techniques other than inspection are used. Inspection can be performed at the supplier's plant prior to shipment or it can be performed at the buyer's plant after receipt of the goods. In some cases, verification might have to be done later upon installation into the final product or even during use. It is best that all this be agreed upon by the supplier and buyer when the purchase order becomes final. Some advantages of each method are considered in the following paragraphs.

The amount of inspection also has to be established by the buyer. Engineering and quality control, working with the purchasing department, decide which characteristics to inspect or test and how many items are to undergo each check. The number of items to check depends on several factors. The importance of each characteristic must be considered. The cost of checking and difficulty of performing each inspection or test are also important considerations. If the items are destroyed or damaged by the test, this also creates a limitation. Sometimes the buyer does not have the necessary test or inspection equipment to perform all of the checks upon receipt. Each of these factors is considered in planning for the inspection and test for each type of item purchased from suppliers.

Especially careful or thorough inspection is needed in several cases as follows:

1. Considerable labor is to be subsequently expended on the item.
2. The item goes into an assembly, and the entire assembly will be lost or expensive rework results if the item is found to be defective.
3. The item cannot be readily evaluated later and eventual product function or salability is affected.
4. Defectives may seriously affect manufacturing operations.
5. Safety of workers or of customers may be jeopardized by defectives.
6. Items cannot be returned for credit later because of the terms of the purchase order.

INSPECTION UPON RECEIPT OF GOODS

When a purchase order has been given to a supplier, it is important to make sure that the methods of inspection have been defined. Upon arrival of the goods at the buyer's receiving dock, the exact procedures for test and inspection can then be implemented without delay. Ideally, these inspection or test methods have been correlated with those of the supplier.

Upon receipt, the goods are identified and the quantity determined before inspection starts. It is necessary to have a copy of the purchase order at hand for use in establishing the applicable requirements. Sometimes shipments will have to be set aside until the inspection or test is ready to be started. In some cases a sample will be removed from the shipment and sent to a laboratory for testing; in other cases each item is checked. Often, a sample from the lot is inspected to establish the acceptability of the entire lot.

Prompt checking for conformance is important, since delays can have legal implications. Delay in performing inspection can also cause production problems in cases where the items are needed to keep lines moving. Delays can also result in items accumulating and becoming mixed up or difficult to control. Control charts have been used effectively to identify excessive processing times. The charts have been effectively used when the production department has accused the quality control department of unnecessary delays in inspection. The charts may establish that the average inspection times are less than the delays on the receiving dock.

RESPONSIBILITIES UPON RECEIPT OF GOODS

Upon receipt of goods, responsibilities can be divided into two categories. One function, usually the responsibility of the quality control department, is to ascertain that the goods conform to the requirements. The other function involves physical receipt, identification, and movement of goods to stores or to the place of next usage, as well as notification of appropriate internal company personnel. The notification to accounting may await inspection to assure conformance to the purchase order requirements before payment is made to the supplier.

While the goods are in the receiving area, protection against pilferage must be provided, as well as against unauthorized use prior to completion of inspection. Where goods are determined to be nonconforming, they must be segregated in a secure area to avoid inadvertent use.

It is also important to notify the purchasing department promptly upon receipt of goods so that purchasing records will be updated to show that goods have been received. The proper identification of goods upon receipt is important from the quality standpoint as well as for other reasons. The received goods must be matched to the proper purchase order so that inspection personnel will know which requirements apply to each particular shipment. Any test data or other quality information furnished by the supplier with the shipment can be placed with the goods.

It is also the responsibility of the receiving group (usually not quality control) to determine the quantity received. This information is also of importance to inspection personnel, since sample sizes to be inspected or tested depend upon the lot size received. The purchasing department also needs to know the quantity received in order to determine whether the order is complete, since partial shipments are frequently received. Sometimes the received material is identified only by the supplier's catalog description, and it is essential that it be further identified upon receipt to permit proper disposition and inspection. In many firms this receipt and recording is handled using an on-line computer system, which also can be used to record quality information.

RESULTS OF INSPECTION
AND TESTS

After tests or inspections have been completed on any lot or shipment of supplier goods, a record or report is prepared. The record shows the inspections and tests conducted and the results. Sometimes the results are recorded on the purchase order or other standard record form. It is important that the quality control department retain a copy of the results in case any repetitive problems arise in the future. It is also important that purchasing receive a copy of the results so that the supplier can be informed of any nonconformance found. Favorable results may be used to authorize payment to the supplier. The purchasing agent can do this by forwarding the authorization for payment to the accounting department.

If the test or inspection shows that the goods fail to comply with any of the requirements, one of two actions may result. Either the whole shipment can be returned to the supplier, or— if the discrepancy is minor—the buyer may consult with production, engineering, and quality control to determine if the items might be repaired or even used as they are. Some facilities have a material review board to establish this usability. This review may result in use of all or part of the items in the shipment. Any costs involved due to the nonconformities will have to be negotiated with the supplier. An urgent need for the items in production may provide a reason for not returning them to the supplier. In any case, it is important that corrective action be taken to prevent suppliers from shipping additional items with the same problems.

ALTERNATIVES FOR HANDLING NONCONFORMING ITEMS

When it has been determined that all or part of a shipment received from a supplier does not conform to the quality standards or requirements, several alternatives are available to the buyer. Each requires coordination and approval from other departments, such as engineering, quality control, and production— and sometimes from the customer of the final product. It is also important to communicate with the supplier concerning any contemplated action. Comments or recommendations from personnel performing the inspection, which are made available with the test results, can often be very helpful. The buyer's final decision should consider past quality history of the supplier and whether or not this same defect has occurred in previous shipments. The following alternatives are available.

Complete Rejection. The purchaser has the option of returning nonconforming goods to the supplier. This is usually the best alternative unless the defects are minor or some or all of the items are critically needed and can be made usable. Papers are prepared by the purchasing department to return the goods at the supplier's expense. The supplier should be notified prior to return, since sometimes the supplier may choose to have the defective goods disposed of or shipped to another destination rather than returned. The purchasing agent also must decide whether the supplier should send a replacement shipment of correct conforming goods or whether the order is being terminated due to default by the supplier. The agent may then procure the items elsewhere. The supplier's invoice will not be processed for payment. A supplier who has already been paid can be billed for the returned items. If replacement from the same supplier is expected, the return is documented in case there are any questions about shipments in the future.

Repair. With the concurrence of engineering and quality control, it may be feasible to repair the nonconforming items received from the supplier. In some cases the supplier may elect to send representatives to the buyer's facility to make the repairs or modifications, at the supplier's own expense. A supplier who makes such a repair is then fully aware of the discrepancy and the costs involved. If the buyer were to have company people perform the repairs, negotiations with the supplier to recover costs may result in differences of opinion. Also, when the supplier performs the repairs or modifications, the buyer later can reject the items if they still are not satisfactory. If the buyer handles the repairs, the supplier may contend that any problems turning up later are a result of the repair work done by the buyer's personnel. In either case, the buyer may seek a price reduction for the repaired goods.

Several other factors are important when nonconforming supplier goods are found. The purchasing agent must consult with the other departments involved in the decision. The supplier must be made aware of the rejection promptly. All returns or other actions must be documented for records and control and for use in keeping track of vendor quality histories. This approach will best satisfy both the business needs and quality needs of the buyer's company.

Use "As Is." If the defects are minor, the purchasing agent may secure approval of engineering and quality control to use the material "as is." The supplier should still be made aware of nonconformance, and the fact that it could have been rejected. The shipment should still go on the supplier's record as not conforming to the requirements.

Partial Rejection. The buyer, with approval from engineering and quality control, may decide to reject a portion of the shipment. The part retained may be used "as is" or repaired, depending on the defect. The lot would still be considered as nonconforming for supplier rating purposes.

NONCONFORMING GOODS— LEGAL ASPECTS

Upon receipt of goods from the supplier, the contractor goes through some type of inspection or test to determine if the goods are acceptable. The Uniform Commercial Code (UCC) says that acceptance cannot occur until the buyer has had a reasonable chance to inspect the goods. The inspections may or may not include checks for all the requirements. On the basis of these checks, the contractor may determine that the goods do not conform to one or more of the requirements. The UCC says that the company receiving the nonconforming goods may take one of the three actions: (1) the whole shipment can be rejected, (2) the whole shipment can be accepted, or (3) any unit or units in the lot can be accepted and the remainder rejected.

Whichever action is selected, further remedies can still be sought from the supplier. For example, the contractor could accept four items from the nonconforming lot, send the remaining twenty back to the supplier, and still sue the supplier for breach of contract. A company might take that action if it badly needed the four items and was able to repair them to make them usable. The company might then sue for the repair costs and also damages suffered because conforming items were not available.

Any action taken by the procuring company must be in good faith. Note also that the UCC refers to units. If the purchase order was for fifty drums of oil, the contractor would not be justified in accepting part of a drum. In any dispute, the purchase order will be consulted to ascertain what constitutes a unit. It would also be wise for any inspection or sampling plans to be consistent with the units expressed in the purchase order. This is another important reason why quality control personnel should work with the buyer before the purchase order is placed. The best way to avoid any controversy, however, is for the supplier and contractor to agree on all terms of the subcontract and also on the procedure for inspection as part of the terms of the purchase order.

If receiving inspection finds the lot to be nonconforming, does that constitute rejection? An acceptance or rejection becomes effective only when the supplier has knowledge of it. In the notification, the buyer must clearly state the defect found. At that time, the supplier can make disposition of the rejected lot. The supplier may repair the defect or find another customer who can use the nonconforming goods. This means that the buyer may not be able to change his or her mind and accept the shipment if it has once been rejected and the supplier has been notified of the rejection.

For the buyer to preserve rights, any rejection or acceptance must be clear and timely. Continued silence on the part of the buyer may constitute acceptance after a reasonable time. If there is a rejection, it then becomes the supplier's responsibility to specify disposition of the rejected goods within a reasonable period of time. Very often the buyer's use of the goods can be considered acceptance unless there has been clear communication to the supplier specifying otherwise. Much depends on the contract language and the written communications by the two parties.

In one case that came to court, the buyer purchased production equipment to be installed in a facility operated by a lessee. The contract stated that the buyer's obligation to pay was conditional on the satisfaction of the lessee. When the goods arrived, the lessee notified the supplier that the equipment was unsatisfactory and asked that it be removed. A supplier's representative visited the plant and made some adjustments. The representative later testified that the equipment was in use and working properly when he left the plant.

After the first production run, the vendor was again notified of defects. More adjustments followed, but the lessee couldn't get a satisfactory production run and stopped using the equipment. When the supplier sued for price, the buyer pleaded that there was no acceptance of the goods. The trial court ruled for the vendor, but the buyer appealed. The appellate court found that there was no evidence of the lessee's signifying that the equipment was conforming, or would be retained despite its nonconformity. The court further ruled that the acts of the lessee were neither inconsistent with the contract nor with the seller's continued ownership.

In another case, the contract specified that the goods were to be picked up at the supplier's plant. The supplier notified the buyer that they were ready, but the buyer neither picked them up nor rejected them. In the lawsuit, the buyer pointed out that by terms of the contract, title did not pass until the items were paid for. The court held that title was independent of acceptance—and the buyer had accepted the goods because he had not rejected them.

Revoking Acceptance. What if the buyer accepted a shipment of goods and then changed his or her mind? Again, it is important that the contract terms define the point of acceptance. Any preliminary or conditional acceptance should be stated as such. The UCC gives protection to the seller, and when acceptance is given by the buyer in accordance with the terms of the purchase order, a subsequent rejection will not usually be enforceable. The UCC does, however, allow revocation of an acceptance under certain conditions as follows:

1. The goods do not conform to the specified requirements.
2. The value to the buyer of the supplier's goods is reduced substantially due to a nonconformance.
3. It was difficult to determine the nonconformance.
4. The supplier provided assurance that the requirements were met.
5. The buyer had reason to assume that the supplier was going to correct the nonconformance.

In any of these situations, the buyer must notify the supplier within a reasonable time after the nonconformity is discovered. Also, the revocation must be made before there is any substantial change in the goods not caused by their own defects.

On some occasions a supplier will agree to a purchase order specifying that the buyer must be satisfied with the goods. Even though the goods conform to the requirements, the vendor has agreed to the terms allowing the buyer to return them. A court will uphold the buyer's right to return goods in these cases, but the buyer has the burden to prove that the terms are in the agreement.

Quality control engineers and inspectors should have an understanding of these legal aspects of the Uniform Commercial Code in order to carry out inspection responsibilities in a way that does not jeopardize the rights or assets of the company. The UCC provides that the receiving company's rejection must be within a "reasonable" time after delivery. Again, the term "rejection" includes notification to the supplier, but does not require the buyer to return the goods, even if the buyer had indicated that they would be returned. Once the goods are rejected, it is the supplier's responsibility to take action for their disposition. If the contractor does not reject and notify the supplier within a reasonable time, the right to do so later may be forfeited. This is true unless acceptance is stated as conditional or the purchase order allows acceptance or rejection at a later point—such as after assembly into a product where the fit can be verified. This again emphasizes the need for close coordination between quality personnel and purchasing personnel as the decisions to reject or accept are made and disposition of material is established.

SUPPLIER-FURNISHED DATA

It is the responsibility of the purchasing department to procure items meeting the quality standards and requirements. This includes the responsibility to assure that quality requirements are met without excessive cost. In many cases these objectives can be best achieved if the supplier sends the results of the test that has been conducted along with the goods. Although this data may not be used as the sole basis for acceptance by the buyer, it is often of considerable value. In some instances receiving inspection may verify the supplier's data on a spot-check basis. In other cases receiving inspection may compare its inspection results with the vendor's data. If there are any differences, the data serves as a base from which to work with the supplier and more quickly establish reasons for the difference.

In some cases the supplier may use process control charts to assure quality. Process control charts and their interpretation are covered in a separate section of this chapter. Copies of the charts might be sent along with the shipment by the supplier as evidence that the goods conform to the requirements. Process control charts would be applicable to chemicals, wire, yarn, or other materials manufactured in a continuous process. The buyer might still, however, check a sample upon receipt of the shipment. The practice of requiring the supplier to send actual test results or other data provides much greater assurance to the buyer than merely asking for a certificate stating that all requirements are met. In addition, the data can be used by the buyer's quality control or engineering personnel for evaluation or to help resolve any problems that occur later in assembly or after shipment of the final product.

EFFECTIVE USE OF
SUPPLIER QUALITY DATA

The procuring company can achieve both cost savings and added quality assurance through the systematic use of vendor-supplied data. Initially, the supplier furnishes the test or inspection data with each shipment. If only a sample is checked by the supplier, it might be packed separately from the rest of the lot. The buyer can then perform similar tests or inspections on the same sample and compare results with those furnished by the supplier. If there are differences, they must be investigated and resolved, but this can be accomplished faster if both parties have checked the same items.

As the buyer develops confidence in the supplier's ability to control processes, hold tolerances, and perform tests, the amount of checking performed by the buyer can be reduced. The buyer can rely more on the supplier and perform spot checks on a monitoring basis. If any discrepancies do turn up, it may be necessary to reinstitute more inspection as well as to require corrective action from the supplier. In general, the use of data provides both cost savings and further assurance of quality conformance.

INSPECTION AT SOURCE

Inspection at the supplier's plant prior to shipment is called "source inspection," or vendor surveillance. Sometimes source inspection implies actual inspection, in which the buyer sends inspectors to the supplier's plant to perform the inspection. In other instances, the buyer's representative may witness the supplier's tests or ask for data showing test results. There are several reasons for utilizing source inspection.

1. The inspection equipment is not available at the buyer's facility, either due to its high cost or for other reasons.
2. The purchase order specifies acceptance at the supplier's facility.
3. Inspection or tests can best be performed during manufacture, such as by use of process control charts.
4. It is desirable to avoid the costs of returning shipments, especially if the goods are costly to ship, the shipping distance is great, or the schedule would not tolerate a delay.
5. The goods are to be shipped directly to the using customer or to a field use site without going to the buyer's facility.
6. There have been frequent quality problems in the past.

7. With cost-plus contracts, it is logical for the buyer to assist the supplier in preventing the production of non-conforming items.
8. The buyer does not have trained personnel to perform the tests or inspection.

The policy of inspecting at source is widely used by the Department of Defense and by other contractors when one or more of these factors are present.

In order for source inspection to be successful, the buyer must delegate authority to the personnel performing the source inspection. These source inspectors may need training in inspection and testing, and they also should have knowledge of the function of the supplied items and the final products using the items. In some cases it may be necessary for the source inspection personnel to communicate with technical people back at the buyer's plant to resolve any technical questions before final acceptance at source is authorized. Any resulting delay that may be caused by difficulties in communicating the results can make source inspection less desirable.

The quantity of items ordered and value of goods purchased must also be sufficient to justify keeping the buyer's inspectors at the supplier facility on a continuing basis. One alternative is to have the supplier notify the buyer when the goods are ready to be inspected so that someone can be sent to the supplier facility.

The costs of inspection should be considered as part of the costs of the supplied material. If source inspection is to be required, the buyer may need to consider distance from the buyer's plant as a factor when suppliers are being evaluated. If several types of items are being procured from the same supplier, or from suppliers in the same location, costs of source inspection may be reduced. An itinerant inspector is defined as an inspector who drops in at a supplier's plant occasionally. The inspector may have the responsibility for inspection of several suppliers in a general area. This is in contrast to the resident inspector, who permanently resides at the supplier facility. In some cases, resident quality control or test engineers must be utilized to monitor complex products and testing prior to shipment. This is true more often for complex equipment.

DUTIES OF
THE SOURCE INSPECTOR

Responsibilities will be assigned to the source inspection personnel based on the nature of the product, past quality history, and the nature of the specified requirements. The following are examples of activities that may be assigned to source inspection personnel:

1. First-piece inspection or monitoring of final tests performed by the supplier in accordance with the specification
2. Checking test or inspection data or reports, and possibly the sign-off of each report if the test was witnessed
3. Keeping buyer's purchasing department advised of possible delays due to schedule delays or quality problems at the supplier facility; providing early warnings of possible technical problems that might occur after delivery
4. Assuring that failed items or failure reports returned to the supplier are properly followed up to determine causes of the failure, assuring that corrective action is taken by supplier to prevent further failures
5. Monitoring the supplier's quality control system and procedures to make sure they are being followed
6. Participating in the review of nonconforming items being considered for use (Some facilities use a Material Review Board to make the decisions); the source inspector would act for the buyer, coordinating with people back at the plant where necessary

7. Monitoring qualification tests performed at the supplier facility
8. Monitoring in-process quality controls used in manufacture
9. Ascertaining that design changes are approved and incorporated at the proper time as specified by the purchase order
10. Accepting goods at the supplier plant for the buyer when authorized to do so, rejecting material that does not conform

Persons performing source inspection should be selected on the basis not only of technical competence, but also of their ability to deal effectively with supplier personnel. They must understand their responsibilities as agents of the buyer, as well as the limitations on their activities. It is usually desirable to transfer source inspection personnel periodically so that personal relationships do not become too close.

SURVEILLANCE OF THE VENDOR'S OPERATIONS

As part of source inspection, the buyer's representative should look at the supplier's overall operations. The following are some guidelines for doing this:

1. Make sure that quality objectives are in agreement with supplier's company objectives.
2. Check to see if the quality control people work with and motivate people in other parts of the supplier organization.
3. Determine whether preventive activities are taken by quality control before production starts.
4. Does the supplier have a continuous evaluation of products and activities?

5. Does the supplier have well-defined standards for all products?
6. Are corrective actions taken when rejections occur, in order to prevent further occurrence of the problems?
7. A good data collection and record system is necessary for an effective quality control program. When defects recur, the records are needed.

PROCESS CONTROLS

The source inspector often has the responsibility for surveillance of the supplier's processes. Statistical techniques can be applied to matching operations or other repetitive processes. Some basic concepts that would be helpful in source inspection tasks are illustrated here.

Variation: Items manufactured in a machining or other manufacturing process are not all exactly alike. Each measurable dimension will vary to some extent on either side of the nominal value. Usually the variation is in the form of a normal curve. Since these variations are very small (perhaps as small as a few thousandths of a centimeter), the parts may appear to the naked eye to be identical. Precision gauges or test equipment, however, can show the differences. An objective of a quality control system is to control variation so the specified tolerances are not exceeded.

Variation occurs in three different ways. A particular dimension can differ slightly from one item to the next. We will call this the item-to-item variation. There can also be variation in a particular characteristic within a piece. For example, diameter may vary along the length of the rod.

The third type of variation can occur, for example, on a time basis. As a tool wears from usage, a resulting machined dimension may become greater. Variation can result from a variety of causes. The first possible cause is the process itself, such as the machine and tool. The raw material can also vary and be the cause of variation in the product. People are the cause of the third possible variation, such as variation due to the operator of the machine. Other factors such as temperature of humidity can also cause variation in a dimension.

Any process has some inherent variation due to chance. Other variation is due to an *assignable cause,* such as an incorrect setting or tool wear. It is an objective of quality control to be able to identify when an assignable cause exists so that a process can be corrected. This requires the separation of the assignable causes from the chance causes of variation, since the chance causes are expected.

Process Control Charts. A control chart provides a graphic presentation of the variation in a process. The typical process control chart would plot readings as a particular dimension or other characteristics being measured. The diameter of a machined part is an example. A control chart for the diameter of a part is illustrated in figure 6-1.

For this particular chart, a sample of five parts is taken each hour, where the production rate is approximately 100 per hour. The diameters of the five parts are measured, and the sample mean of the five is calculated and plotted on the chart. If the upper (UCL) or lower (LCL) limit is exceeded, the variation is greater than that due to chance alone. If either limit is exceeded, the operation is stopped until the cause of the excessive variation is determined. In the case illustrated the tool had become loose and was reset.

While there are several types of control charts, some of which plot other than the mean value, the principle of stopping the process if the limit is exceeded always applies.

Examine each of the process control charts in figure 6-2. Assume that you observe each one in a supplier's process. Answer the following for each chart:

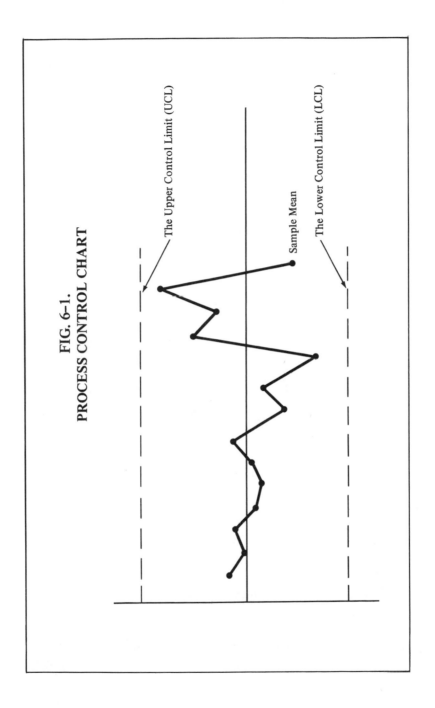

FIG. 6–1.
PROCESS CONTROL CHART

The Upper Control Limit (UCL)

Sample Mean

The Lower Control Limit (LCL)

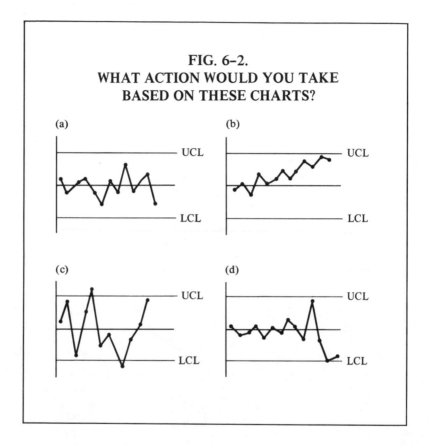

FIG. 6–2.
WHAT ACTION WOULD YOU TAKE
BASED ON THESE CHARTS?

(a)

UCL

LCL

(b)

UCL

LCL

(c)

UCL

LCL

(d)

UCL

LCL

1. Is an assignable cause present?
2. Would you recommend that the process be stopped?
3. What is a possible cause of the problem, if one exists?
4. Can you make any suggestions?

Chart *a* shows that the process is in control. In Chart *b*, although the limit has not been exceeded, it appears that it soon will be, due to the continuous trend. The process should be stopped immediately before any defective items are produced.

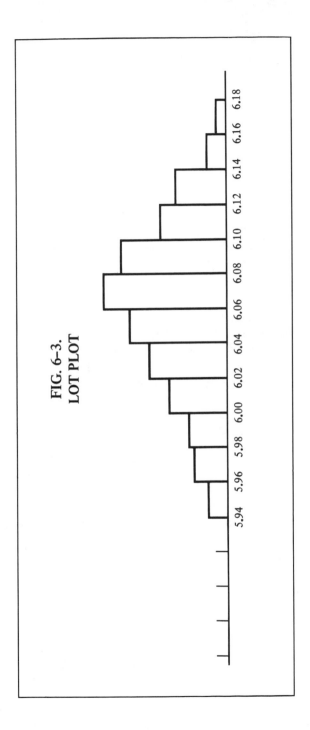

FIG. 6–3.
LOT PLOT

Since the trend is gradual, tool wear is a possible cause. The tool could be set between the central line and the LCL. This would be better than resetting to the central line, since a reset to below the central line will allow more wear before measurements again become close to the UCL. Chart *c* indicates both control limits have been exceeded. There are no trends. A loose tool could cause this type of situation. The process should have been stopped when the upper control limit was first exceeded. In chart *d*, the first ten points plotted on the chart stayed close to the nominal. Although neither limit has been exceeded, the sudden increase in variation should arouse concern. It is recommended that the cause of the increased variation be investigated.

Lot Plot. When the parts being produced by a machine are measured and the measurements recorded in a plot as pictured in figure 6-3, we call this a "lot plot." The lot plot can tell us the capability of the machine to hold the tolerance, whether the machine is set properly, and if there appears to be something causing the measurements to be out of control. In figure 6-3, it appears that the machine has the ability to hold the tolerance, but that it is set so that the nominal falls on 6.06 rather than 6.00.

Normal Distribution. It has been well established that most machines and processes yield dimensions or other characteristics in the form of a normal curve as shown in figure 6-4. If a machine were set to turn a shaft of 6 cm in diameter, we know that all shafts would not be exactly the same. The precision of the machine would determine how close the variation could be held. From past experience we might know that the parts would fall in a distribution as pictured with *almost* 100 percent of the items being within ± .120 cm of the mean value at which the machine is set.

Normal curve theory actually establishes that 99.7 percent of the parts will fall within three standard deviations of the mean.

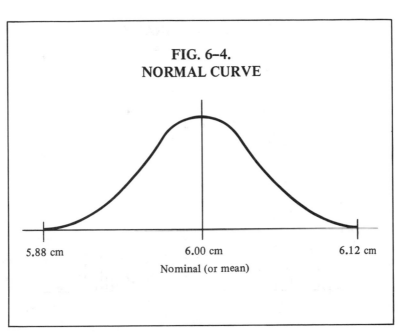

FIG. 6–4.
NORMAL CURVE

5.88 cm   6.00 cm   6.12 cm

Nominal (or mean)

In the case pictured, three standard deviations equal .120 and one standard deviation would be .040.

Tolerances. If the drawing specified 6.00 ± .24 cm, the tolerance would be .24 cm in either direction from the nominal value. The machine could easily hold this tolerance if set at the nominal (6.00). If the drawing specified 6.00 ± .09 cm, we can see that due to the limited natural capability of the machine, it could not hold all of the parts produced within the tolerance. It would be necessary to select a better machine, which could hold a tighter tolerance.

Examples for Analysis. Each of the lot plots in figure 6-5 was made from a sample of fifty items. Assume that each sample of

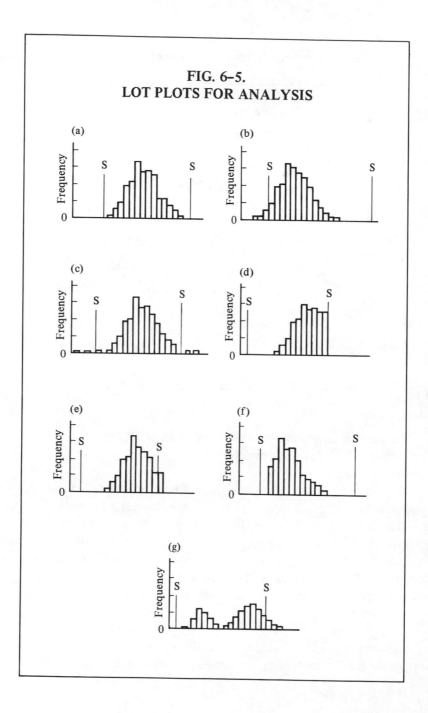

FIG. 6–5.
LOT PLOTS FOR ANALYSIS

fifty was taken from a different lot of material received from the supplier. Make a preliminary analysis of each lot plot based on your observation. Specification limits are shown by S.

Possible evaluations of each lot plot are given below:

a. This plot can be expected from a normal distribution process with all parts within the specification limit.
b. The process would be able to hold the specification limits if the nominal were set to the right.
c. The machine or process has too much natural variation and—although it appears normal—points on both ends of the distribution are out of the specified limits.
d. It appears that the process was not set on the correct nominal and that parts not within limits were sorted out of the lot.
e. Same as (d), except that the gauge used in sorting was not set correctly and defectives are present.
f. Same as (e), except the gauge was set in a way that rejected some good items.
g. It appears that parts from two different lots have been mixed together. One lot does not meet the requirements.

Actual Case. A company was planning to procure item "X," where a diameter was critical and particularly difficult to machine. Two suppliers each claimed to be able to meet the requirement. The buyer ordered five hundred parts from each supplier as a trial to determine ability to meet the specification requirement. Upon receipt, the items from each supplier were carefully inspected and were within specified tolerance. The buyer then had the measurements of each supplier recorded in a lot plot as shown in figure 6-6. From the lot plots he concluded that Supplier *A* produced five hundred items, all within specifications, by a controlled process. He also concluded that Supplier *B* sorted out and submitted five hundred items within the limits.

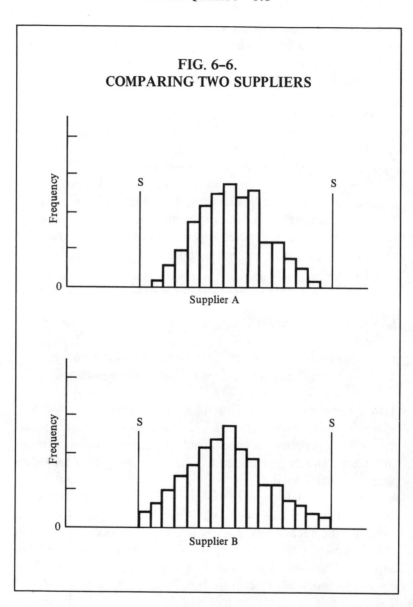

FIG. 6–6.
COMPARING TWO SUPPLIERS

It was apparent to the buyer that if orders were given to B, costly 100 percent inspection would be required, and some out-of-tolerance items might get shipped. Supplier A, however, seemed able to produce all good items under a controlled process, and should be given the order.

INSPECTION
AND TEST

Quality Control can be separated into two tasks: *control of quality* (defect prevention) and *verification of quality*. Inspection and test fall primarily into the second category. Verification implies that inspection or test must be performed to measure one or more characteristics of the product. In this chapter we deal with inspection and test as they apply to supplier-furnished products, materials, and services.

PLANNING FOR INCOMING
INSPECTION AND TEST

For each item to be purchased, someone must decide what type of person—possessing what skills, and using what equipment—is necessary to verify that the item is satisfactory. This inspection or test can be performed at the supplier's or at the buyer's facility.

In conjunction with this decision, someone must also decide at what level or combinations of levels to make inspections and tests. They can be performed on parts, assemblies, completed product, or combinations of products assembled into a system. The decision of what and when to test is a matter of both economics and technical feasibility. Usually it is desirable to make inspections or tests as early as possible, preferably as the item is being manufactured. This permits making corrections to a process whenever there is evidence that the process is not in control. Sometimes, however, a characteristic cannot be measured until items are assembled together into components or assemblies. Normally we prefer to avoid having to dismantle components or assemblies in order to remove and replace defective items. Much production and assembly work can be automated, but rework and repair must be handled on an individual basis and therefore become costly. We might conclude it is best to set the objective of locating defectives at the lowest possible level.

INVESTIGATING THE PRODUCT

Upon receipt of a shipment, little information is available to the inspector concerning how a supplier part was fabricated, so performing the incoming inspection can become difficult. The quality planner must recognize the resulting pitfalls and provide ease of inspection as well as protection to the user. To achieve a satisfactory degree of protection against defects, the individual providing the planning must investigate the part thoroughly. In order to simplify the approach, basic inspection concepts can be categorized by commodity types. For example, the categories might include printed circuit boards, hardware, stampings, castings, turned parts, chemicals, software, processes, etc. If aligned with the purchasing department's breakdown of products, the planning can be done while working with the vendor during initial contacts. This basic planning includes identification of the characteristics critical to the function of the product.

While investigating a part in the development of the inspection plan, a knowledge of the vendor's manufacturing technique and familiarity with the strengths or weaknesses of the manufacturing approach are helpful. For example, knowing that flash and "knit" lines in plastic moldings are indicators of potentially out-of-control conditions on tooling temperature or pressures would assist in developing a good plan. Knowing that a supplier has several machines producing the same part becomes a basis for developing the correct sample sizes or sampling approach. This knowledge should also be used to establish requirements to the supplier with respect to segregation and identification of material. If properly segregated, stratified sampling or sampling by production machine or tool cavity can be accomplished.

Establishing a checklist that can be used in inspection or tests is effective in assuring that the plan is effective. These checks should include:

- Method used to produce the item
  - ☐ Is the method prone to error?
  - ☐ Is the method variable?
  - ☐ Are there visual or easily measured values that can be used in verification?
  - ☐ Does each characteristic need to be measured?

- How many machines are producing the part?

- Is the tooling permanent?

- Is there more than one cavity?

- Are there secondary operations?
  - ☐ Any holes requiring tapping?
  - ☐ Surfaces need buffing?

- Is the process active and does it require continuous attention to maintain stability?
  - ☐ When are additions made?
  - ☐ How are additions specified?
  - ☐ What method is used to verify additions?

- How can software be tested?
  - ☐ What system changes need to be anticipated?

- How can a random sample be selected?

- Can the characteristic be measured automatically or with instrumentation?

- How is supplied item used?

- How many are used in each assembly?

- What impact will a defect have?
  - □ Will the defect be detectable during use of part?
  - □ Will the defect be detectable during subsequent application in the product?
  - □ Will the defect be detectable prior to providing the end product to the customer?
  - □ What is the cost for rework of a defect?
  - □ Can the defect be reworked or will it result in scrap?
  - □ What impact will the defect have on production flow?
  - □ How will the defect affect the reliability and function of product?

- Will the sampling plan provide the needed protection?

- How many parts are received per lot?

- How often are lots received?

Sampling plans are often ineffective as a way of identifying defects that can have serious results on production flows. For example: If a product uses one hundred devices in each product and the devices are received with a 1 percent defective level, it is likely that on the average, every product in flow will have at least one defective device in it. Further, if the devices are inspected using a 1.5 percent AQL, the material will most likely always be accepted. Obviously this is a special situation requiring evaluation and resolution, but it illustrates an important point.

After establishing answers to the checklist of questions above, an appropriate plan can be developed. The analysis may demonstrate the need to inspect one supplier's product differently than another's. If this is the case, the plan should clearly indicate how this is to be accomplished. Revisions to the plan can be easily made and incorporated based on either good or bad product performance. If the product performs well, reduced inspection might be allowed. If a defect is found, revision of inspection criteria must be promptly made.

Once completed, the inspection plan should be evaluated with an incoming lot to determine how well it works, both as to effectiveness and practicality. An inspection plan calling for a 1.5 percent AQL on all dimensions of a part having two hundred separate characteristics could easily require sixteen to twenty hours per part, and the better part of a month to do the complete lot. Unless the manpower is provided for this type of inspection, an alternate method must be developed.

TESTING

Regardless of whether we are dealing with parts, components, assemblies, or entire systems, the purpose of a test is to ascertain if the item functions as required in the specified environment. To accomplish the purpose, the person responsible for planning the testing must have a complete understanding of the item to be tested, its function, how it is to be used, and the environment in which it is to function. For any item, there will be tests that are unique to it. However, there will also be tests that are traditional for items falling into a generic grouping.

Generic Tests. There are certain tests that can be applied to many types of products using general test equipment. For example, a product may need to operate under certain temperature conditions. The temperature range may vary from item to item, but a standard environmental test chamber can be used to conduct the tests.

Generic tests can be grouped as follows:

1. *Environmental*—Testing under the temperature, humidity, pressure, vibration, or shock conditions it is expected to endure in shipment, storage, and actual use
2. *Acoustic or electromagnetic conditions*
3. *Reliability*—To determine if the product operates over a period of time without failure
4. *Safety*—To verify that the user will not be injured while the product is in use or is being placed in service

Unique Tests. Certain tests are to verify characteristics peculiar to the product. These tests can be grouped as follows:

1. *Functional*—To determine if the item performs as required
2. *Maintainability*—To determine if the product can be serviced or repaired readily using available documentation and tools
3. *Appearance factors and product identification markings*
4. *Physical measurements*

DIFFICULTIES IN RECEIVING INSPECTION

Inspection of a product at receiving is one of the most difficult tasks to perform. Little information is available to indicate the critical factors important to doing a good inspection. In-process checks that are important to control the final quality characteristics cannot be done since the product is completed when received. More than one lot of raw material or more than one machine's output may be represented by a particular lot. Material fabricated or produced at different times may be included in a lot. The product may be packaged to protect it from handling damage or the environment and may be bulky, heavy, or messy—or any number of other conditions may exist to present an inspector with difficulties. Yet the receiving inspector's responsibility is to assure that defective material is rejected, acceptable material is accepted, and that every possible interpretation of the requirements are known, understood, and applied. Regardless of the situation, accepting rejectable material and rejecting acceptable material is costly to both the supplier and user in terms of schedules, manpower, and profit margins. Neither condition can be allowed to exist long without resulting in serious problems.

Commodity Similarities. Physical characteristics can restrain effective inspection. The material may be delivered in a train tank car, tractor trailer, or be corrosive, explosive, or temperature-sensitive. Or it could be so tiny as to require high magnification to see. In each case, a method of handling and processing material must be developed to assure an effective inspection. One approach is to establish guidelines for receiving inspection consistent with the type of commodity involved. In general, inspection approaches are similar for a commodity grouping. A typical commodity listing could include the following:

RAW CHEMICALS
STEEL
PRECIOUS METALS
HARDWARE (SCREWS/NUTS/BOLTS)
PRINTED CIRCUIT BOARDS
ELECTRONIC COMPONENTS
    (RESISTORS, DIODES, MICROCHIPS)
ELECTRONIC ASSEMBLIES
SOFTWARE (PROGRAMS)
DIE-CAST PARTS
SHEET METAL
PAINTED PARTS
MOTORS
TRANSFORMERS

Each of these groups could have generic inspection criteria. For instance, the generic requirements for a printed circuit board would be: part number; outline (physical size, thickness, shape); hole size; no bridging of conductors; no breaks of conductors; proper plating thickness of contacts; adhesion of marking; location of holes on center (critical for automatic insertion); conductivity of the surface; and solderability. Using the characteristics described, an inspector can perform inspection on received material, and only selected special checks would need to be done to individual lots. However, the inspector should have written instructions detailing special characteristics to be checked on each lot.

Each commodity could easily have a list of characteristics identifying general requirements applying to each lot of material received, thereby maximizing the efficiency of control and minimizing the risk of accepting poor material.

Part Number Verification. Of all the inspections accomplished at receiving inspection, the verifying of proper part number is most common. This is important to control of the material in the production system. If done incorrectly, material will be accepted that is incorrectly identified and can cause trouble later in production. If a part is accepted under the wrong number, it can result in false inventory records that will not support production requirements. It could also result in the mixing of stock, incorrect assemblies, rework, and scrap. Performing electrical and physical inspection might be the only way to verify the correct number for a part, but in any case it must be done accurately.

Appearance. Inspecting a product for appearance is a function likely to cause difficulties between the supplier and user. Acceptability of appearance is dependent upon the judgment of the inspector. For example, parts are often plated with nickel to provide protection and wear characteristics, yet nickel-plated items are often rejected because of poor appearance. The rejections seem to be proportional to the lack of shine. Also, if raw material lines show through, the rejections increase. The more inspection an item receives, the more likely that appearance rejections will occur. Careful control of visual rejections is necessary since the rejections may actually be uncalled for or they may mask an incomplete inspection activity. Caution must be taken to assure that an appearance rejection, which quite often is the first characteristic to be inspected, does not preclude completion of the remainder of the inspection.

In the case of the nickel-plated parts, appearance can be difficult to evaluate. Zinc chromate, if used as a substitute plating, will not have as much of a problem for appearance since it is nonuniform in appearance and color. It might be easier to change the plating material than to train everyone about the appearance criteria.

If the product requires certain appearance characteristics—such as a home appliance—then the criteria for acceptance or rejection should be clear, easy to interpret, understandable, and easily communicated. Often physical samples of acceptable and unacceptable appearance are needed to describe the characteristics. Such physical samples must be protected since handling will affect the samples' appearance and result in a criteria change or invalidation of the inspection.

In some instances acceptance standards are set by a group of typical samples, some acceptable and some unacceptable. This method is used, for example, in the beverage and food industry, where experts establish the appearance, taste, and appeal.

Physical Constraints. In many cases physical constraints prevent or hamper an effective inspection. Sometimes train car or tractor trailer shipments of parts present difficulties in assuring that a random sample is taken. What inspector is not tempted to sample the parts immediately available rather than go through the procedure of taking a random sample? The best alternative might be to inspect parts randomly as they are being moved from the conveying vehicle into the stockroom or to the production line. This system requires good control since rejection of a lot entails capturing the complete lot and holding it in an appropriate location to allow return to the supplier or other disposition.

WHERE TO INSPECT AND
HOW MUCH INSPECTION

Where is the best inspection location from an economic perspective? It is important also to consider the legal aspects that may determine if a shipment is legally accepted or not. The following are guidelines as to where inspections (or tests) should be performed. These guidelines can be used to help determine the appropriate amount of inspection or test upon receipt of goods from suppliers.

1. Inspect or test after operations with low yields, so that costly operations are not later added to already defective products.
2. Inspect or test before operations where relatively high value is added, so that defectives are removed before further value is added.
3. Inspect or test before operations that may cover up defects or make defects difficult to find or to repair.
4. Inspect or test at points in the process where it is comparatively inexpensive, such as with automatic test equipment.

In any case, it is important to inspect or test in such a way that the results can be used to control quality and to prevent further defectives. We can apply some of these concepts to determine the amount of inspection or test to be performed upon receipt of the product, by considering the next step in the process. To some extent, the discussion of how much inspection to perform at incoming is really a determination of where to inspect.

AMOUNT OF INCOMING INSPECTION

Several studies have dealt with the amount of incoming inspection that is economically optimum. Even with the number of variables, we can identify some rules of thumb. From a very general viewpoint, there are three choices: (1) no incoming inspection, (2) 100 percent inspection, or (3) acceptance sampling.

Throughout this book we will take the position that the preferred strategy is to ensure that supplied goods are free of defects—and in many cases this is actually a feasible strategy. If we use acceptance sampling, the implication is that a certain percentage of defects is acceptable, and the buyer will probably get that percentage in the supplied goods. The third alternative is 100 percent inspection upon receipt. Human error prevents this method from being perfect. We may, however, achieve 100 percent effective inspection or testing with automatic test equipment.

With these thoughts in mind, a company may decide it wants 100 percent good items upon receipt. However, that goal is not reasonably attainable. The question then is, should 100 percent testing be performed upon receipt, or should no testing be performed and the failed items removed and replaced later in the assembled product? To respond to this question, where the objective is to perform the economically optimum action, some rough rules of thumb are helpful. The rules set forth here are a much simplified version of those presented by Dr. W. Edward Deming.[1]

1. W. Edward Deming, *Quality, Productivity, and Competitive Position* (Cambridge: MIT Press, 1982).

The following parameters are given:

P = Fraction defective of incoming goods.

K_1 = Cost to inspect (or test) one item.

K_2 = Cost to later remove and replace the item if found defective after assembly into the product.

The rules of thumb are:

$$\text{If } P < \frac{K_1}{K_2}: \text{ perform no test at incoming.}$$

$$\text{If } P > \frac{K_1}{K_2}: \text{ perform 100 percent incoming inspection.}$$

The rule is simple enough. However, the assumption is that a choice is being made based on economics only. We know, however, that there are other considerations besides those expressed by this pair of formulas.

100 PERCENT INSPECTION

Inspecting every item is called 100 percent inspection, or screening. This should result in rejection of all nonconforming items and acceptance of all good items; but it is not that simple. Sampling plans were developed for several reasons:

1. 100 percent inspection is expensive and time consuming.
2. The inadequacy of 100 percent inspection due to human error, monotony, overlooking defects, etc.
3. Lack of incentive on supplier to ship all good items if he knows customer will sort them.
4. Some tests are destructive.

Recently, however, the use of automatic test and inspection equipment has been able to eliminate (1) and (2) above. This means that a buyer, when the supplier claims he uses 100 percent inspection, needs to ascertain just what is being checked and how is it being done, by machine or humans.

ACCEPTANCE SAMPLING

An acceptance sampling plan is applied to a lot (or batch) of items to determine if the items in the lot meet the standards. In acceptance sampling, a sample of predetermined size n is to be taken from a lot of size N. If the number of defectives exceeds the acceptance number c, the lot is rejected. Otherwise the lot is accepted. If we were inspecting a unit, we could count defects per unit rather than number of defectives.

We will deal here only with single sampling (the simplest form) where one sample is taken from each lot and a decision to accept or reject is based on the one sample. Consider an example:

$$N = 500$$
$$n = 50$$
$$c = 3$$

We select a random sample of 50 items from the lot of 500. If 3 or fewer are defective, we accept the lot. If 4 or more defectives are found, we reject the lot.

Advantages of Acceptance Sampling. There are a number of reasons for using acceptance sampling rather than 100 percent inspection as follows:

1. Sampling is more economical, as it requires fewer inspections and thus fewer inspectors.

2. Less product handling takes place, and therefore damage is less likely.
3. Inspection becomes less monotonous, and therefore with fewer items to be inspected, the likelihood of error is reduced.
4. Some inspections or tests are destructive, and in such cases sampling *must* be used.
5. A sampling plan provides a predetermined sample size and acceptance number, based on statistical concepts, and the numbers are not left to inspector judgment.
6. Plans provide for rejection of entire lots if c is exceeded. This provides greater motivation to the producer submitting the lot to submit good quality and take corrective action on rejects.

Disadvantages of Sampling. There are also disadvantages to any sampling plan as follows:

1. There are risks of accepting bad lots and rejecting good lots.
2. Time and expertise are needed to set up valid sampling plans and negotiate them with suppliers.
3. Information available is limited to data from the sample.
4. When entire lots are rejected, production personnel may try to force quality control personnel to sort a shipment to keep production going.

Establishing Lots. The effectiveness and efficiency of sampling is influenced by the way the lots are formed. The following are some rules to establish lots for sampling purposes.

1. Lots should be homogeneous. For example, all items in a lot should be produced in the same batch, by the same machine, same operator, etc.
2. It is more efficient to use as large lots as possible.

3. Lots should be suited to shipping containers, vehicles, and materials handling equipment. For example, a keg or a truckload would be designated as a lot.
4. The selection of the sample should be easily accomplished. Sorting and counting to select the sample is to be avoided.

ADVANCE VS. ON-ARRIVAL SAMPLING

Sometimes a purchaser will arrange to inspect a sample of goods prior to receipt of the shipment. The supplier may ship a selected sample of the material to the buyer. Upon receipt, it is inspected or tested, and the supplier is notified if the results are not acceptable. There are several disadvantages to this type of arrangement.

1. The sample items received may not be representative of the entire lot.
2. Damage or contamination may have occurred during shipment.
3. Unethical practices may have occurred, such as "salting"; that is, adding known defective items to a good lot, while maintaining the percent defective below the limits specified by the purchaser.

A buyer's representative at the supplier facility can alleviate the first and third problems.

Inspection or test on-arrival also has some disadvantages. First and foremost, inspection at the source can eliminate or reduce the receipt of defective lots. Inspection time, delays in start of testing, and holding until acceptance decisions are made are costs to the buying company. There are also the problems related to holding rejected lots for disposition, and associated production problems related to rejected shipments.

SPECIAL CONSIDERATIONS

The following are some special situations that should be dealt with separately in planning for inspection and test.

SOFTWARE

Software is any computer program, and it can be priced and delivered as part of the associated hardware, or separately. It may be loaded as part of the manufacturing process and unalterable, or loadable by the user.

In the control of quality of any product we can speak of the *quality of design*—i.e., does the product meet the needs of the user?—and the *quality of conformance*—i.e., does a particular item conform to the design requirements? Software quality can be evaluated in the same way.

The testing of software for acceptance is essentially the checking of the outputs that the software system generates. The number of possible outputs for the system can be very large, however, and it is hardly possible to check all outputs. This produces a situation in which statistical sampling procedures could apply. If a sample of outputs m is checked and n are acceptable, then the defective rate is $\dfrac{m-n}{m}$. Generally, it is better to take a random sample of the outputs.

As in any supplier quality approach, it is preferable for the test to be performed at the supplier's facility, subject to verification by the purchaser. The test could be witnessed at the supplier facility, or data furnished with the delivered software. Careful planning is required if the software is to be tested upon receipt at incoming inspection.

QUALITY OF SERVICES

The measurement of quality of services is usually more difficult than measuring product quality, but is just as necessary. Important factors in a service are timeliness, accuracy, and completeness of the service performed. Examples of services are security, housekeeping, delivery, or cafeteria service. As with a product, the first step in quality planning is to define what the customer wants; that is, the requirements. Next, possible discrepancies are identified as well as their importance.

Since services are usually labor intensive, attempts to improve productivity will often be at the expense of quality. Just as with products, however, if rework is charged against productivity, no matter how much later the service discrepancy is found, we see that improving quality also enhances productivity.

The feedback of complaints is an important element in measuring quality of a service. It is important to store the data in a manner that allows problems to be easily identified as the data is accumulated, so corrective action can be initiated.

AUTOMATIC TEST EQUIPMENT

Automatic test and inspection equipment has removed many of the major disadvantages previously associated with 100 percent inspection or test. The automatic equipment allows more consistent checking, results in fewer errors, and can be operated at lower per-unit testing cost. Besides the lower cost due to increased speed of checking, the equipment can be operated by less skilled operators.

There are, however, disadvantages related to the use of automatic test equipment. The cost of the equipment is greater—however, for high volume use, the equipment often pays for itself. Also, since automatic test equipment is more complex, failures can result in downtime or costly maintenance.

COMPUTER-AIDED INSPECTION AND TEST

There has been considerable recent progress in the application of computers, along with advanced sensor technology, to automate inspection. Usually the computer-aided inspection is performed on 100 percent of the items and is preferably on-line as part of the production process. This 100 percent on-line inspection provides opportunities to use results of inspection to make compensating adjustments in the manufacturing operation. This results not only in improved product quality, but also in improvement in productivity. In the literature we encounter the terms "computer-aided quality control" (CAQC), "computer-aided test" (CAT), and "computer-aided inspection" (CAI).

The actual automated inspection can be performed with robots equipped with mechanical probes or sensing devices. The use of noncontact sensors is becoming more prevalent, since it reduces the part repositioning required for a contact inspection device. The noncontact sensing devices include optical techniques, electrical inductance or other field measurement, radiation techniques, or methods involving ultrasonics. The noncontact inspection methods also are usually much faster and eliminate potential damage to the part being inspected.

There are different degrees of computer-aided testing. In the more advanced applications, the product is automatically positioned and attached to the testing apparatus. The computer then monitors the test and analyzes, and sometimes records, the results. If the product passes the test, it is automatically moved to the next operation. If it fails the test, it is set aside for further diagnosis and disposition, usually performed manually.

RELIABILITY TESTS

The measurement of reliability is based on how well a supplier's product performs in service after having demonstrated initial acceptable performance. If it fails in service, the product's reliability may be deficient. Reliability failures create problems and considerable concern since they often affect public safety. These defects are the most difficult to trace to an assignable cause since information on the product may not be available or may be difficult to trace. Special reliability tests can be performed as part of qualification tests, or by taking sample items from lots for testing. These tests are designed to catch potential failure before the product goes to the customer.

TEST AND INSPECTION DATA

Results of tests and inspections are the bases for acceptance or rejection of goods. Therefore, the recording of data on the results is important. It serves as backup in case of future questions about the decision and also serves as information to help in solving problems that arise later. The logging and maintenance of inspection and test data are especially important with respect to supplier items. If a lot is rejected, the data serves as substantiation of the rejection if questioned by the supplier. If the goods are accepted, the data becomes very useful in later resolution of problems arising subsequent to the incoming inspection.

In cases where the inspection is performed by the supplier prior to shipment of the goods, data furnished with the shipment can be used to facilitate verification upon receipt. In some cases, the receiver can spot-check by testing specific items and comparing measurements to those furnished by the supplier. The identification of any discrepancies in measurements between purchaser and supplier is helpful in preventing further problems. Sometimes corrections in equipment calibration can be made at this time.

Test data can be either automatically or manually recorded. Automatic test equipment often has strip printers or graphic recording devices. In many cases it is desirable to place a copy of the test results with the product being tested, as well as to retain a copy in file. All data should be dated, written in ink, and signed by the person performing the test or inspection. Any corrected records should not obliterate the erroneous data. All of these reports are important for future quality audits or where problems with the supplier later arise.

Standardized forms for recording data are also important. This helps to ensure that all the required checks are make. It also facilitates later verification of data. For elaborate tests, or acceptance of certain lots of material, it may be necessary to prepare a formal report of the results, possibly including conclusions and/or recommendations. This is especially important to qualification testing.

Inspection records should include:

- part number
- vendor (more than one may be used)
- measurements taken
- tools or instruments used
- sampling plan, if used
- results
- approval status of each vendor
- vendor's identifying number
- drawing or specification revision status
- special notes describing special requirements or measurements

It is unlikely that all characteristics will have the same sampling plan, so a separate space is needed for each characteristic measured. Test and inspection data should be retained for future use if problems occur in production or after shipment to the customer.

PROBLEMS
AND CORRECTIVE
ACTION

Quality-conscious companies need methods to insure that corrective action is taken to remedy problems or correct unsatisfactory conditions. These problems often involve nonconforming goods received from suppliers. We define corrective action as an activity that prevents further occurrence of an unsatisfactory condition. With respect to suppliers, corrective action would assure that further shipments of goods do not contain the nonconformity. Its effectiveness depends on the degree of discipline involved in the methods selected, and can be measured by success in achieving solutions.

Securing successful corrective action on supplier-provided goods is often more difficult than correcting internal problems. This is because factors such as poor communication, differing interpretations of contracts, language differences, and third party involvement interfere with achievement of effective action. Procedures to achieve corrective action with suppliers must be designed to overcome these barriers.

WHAT IS CORRECTIVE ACTION?

Plant personnel often view corrective action as the fix needed to make the nonconforming item usable. This is a dangerous attitude that can delay or negate effective problem solving. In our discussion here, we will define "corrective action" as something done to prevent the repetition of a nonconformity in the future. It will be a permanent solution, not merely action to alleviate the pressure related to accepting a specific lot of material for use. If the corrective action is actually adequate, the particular nonconformity should not appear again. A critical part of any corrective action system is feedback of information to the source of the problem, and follow-up to assure that the problem—or similar problems—will not occur again.

FORMS OF CORRECTIVE ACTION

The following are examples of possible corrective actions that may result from analyses of problems:

1. Design or redesign of tools or fixtures
2. Further training of operator(s)
3. Exhibition of nonconforming items for all to see
4. Changes of process control charts
5. Creation in engineering drawings or other design changes
6. Increased inspection until problem is resolved
7. Revision of material handling methods
8. Changes in material identification
9. Segregation of nonconforming items

EXAMPLES

In each case below assume you are the quality control engineer and have been given proposed corrective actions as a result of defectives found. Evaluate each. Would you accept the corrective action proposed? What additional questions should you ask?

a. A batch of fuel gauges for motorcycles was rejected because about 10 percent of the gauges showed one-quarter full when the tank was empty. Procurement notified the supplier, who provided instructions for adjusting the gauges. This saved the cost of returning the lot.

b. An inspector measured three parts just machined and found all three above the upper tolerance. The operator checked the parts, agreed with the finding, and agreed to take corrective action by replacing a worn tool.

c. When the battery charger on a finished motorcycle did not operate correctly, the tester found the wrong size resistor in a circuit. In checking further he found several more in other units. The assembly department later reported that receiving test had accepted them in spite of the fact that they were marked incorrectly. Incorrect labeling led to inadvertent use in the wrong application. Therefore, the assembly department said quality control should pay for the replacement.

The above actions do not fully constitute corrective action. In problem *a* we should ask:

- Why were the gauges not adjusted properly by the supplier before shipment?
- What was the cost of performing the adjustments at the user plant and who is to pay it?
- What will the supplier do to prevent further shipment of improperly adjusted gauges?

In problem *b:*

- Why didn't the operator know the tool was worn before the inspector noticed it?
- Is there a problem with this tool only, or does the operator check any tools for wear?
- Does the operator have the equipment to check the work?

- Is there an awareness that it is the operator's responsibility to assure quality, and not the inspector's?

Problem c illustrates several user problems, but essentially, the supplier needs to be brought into the problem, and to pay for the rework caused. The attitude of the assembly department is also of concern—punitive action against quality control will not solve the problem.

EVALUATION OF DEFECT

Many companies don't provide the supplier a firsthand opportunity to evaluate the defect. In some cases analysis of the defect or failure is performed without the supplier's participation and perhaps without providing an opportunity to review the discrepancy. This is not only unfair to the supplier, but may also result in delaying the accomplishment of corrective action. On the other hand, prompt action is often advisable, since the supplier may not have the expertise or equipment to perform an adequate evaluation. This occurs when complex analyses of the overall product are required to determine the basic cause of a problem. In other cases, time is of the essence in identifying the problem without disrupting production schedules.

The point is made, however, that regardless of the approach, the vendor should be given the opportunity to evaluate nonconforming goods firsthand and should be provided with all pertinent information on a timely basis. Notifying a vendor of a defect in material many months after it is used causes difficulties for the supplier. Simple conditions such as changes in personnel or production setups may be significant in locating causes of problems. Perhaps a new die designed to meet higher production rates was not used during a low production period, and the substitution resulted in a problem. Timeliness can easily be designed into a corrective action system. The following are some roadblocks to be avoided:

1. Requirement of multiple signing of defect forms before a request for corrective action is made to supplier
2. Requirement that all communications be transmitted through a particular outside agency
3. Requirement of complete defect analysis prior to supplier notification

One company had a corrective action system requiring that several functions as well as customers sign the defect form. It also required the customer to transmit the request for corrective action to the vendor. In one defect notification, the vendor received first notification of the condition eighty-five days after the defect was found and after several thousand parts with similar defects were produced. This resulted in lost production by both supplier and user. Could the corrective action system of your company cause a situation like this?

VENDOR NOTIFICATION

Communication information to the supplier about nonconforming goods is a first step in obtaining corrective action. Yet it is not uncommon to find operations that omit this step. The ailment can take many forms: No formal method may exist for handling defects; parts are not actually returned to the supplier; failures found during assembly are not reported to the functions that should seek corrective action; vendors are not charged for defectives; or no action is taken by purchasing to follow up and correct the nonconformity. Each one of these is an essential step in obtaining effective correction. Company executives often hear a supplier say, "I never heard about the condition," even though the problem has existed for several months. This is not an uncommon occurrence.

Other conditions can also develop: The rejection rate of incoming lots rises to 15 percent; assembly line stoppages occur weekly as a result of defective supplier parts passed through to inventory stock; scrap and rework costs for vendor-caused defects exceed reasonable levels; and sales are lost due to customer complaints about poor material or poor product performance.

These could be described as vendor problems, but they really are the result of poor communication. Most vendors want to perform well. The user must take the first step by communicating effectively with suppliers.

Good communication with suppliers is one key element in achieving corrective action. The method of communication could be any of a variety of alternatives in order to achieve maximum effectiveness. Telephone calls, letters, returned material, visits, and charges back to suppliers should all be used promptly to achieve the desired results. The supplier can be considered an extension of in-plant communications and part of a coordinated effort to achieve corrective action. This approach helps to reduce the number of defective lots received and obtain quicker resolution of discrepancies that do occur.

INTERACTION OF BUYER

In all communications with the supplier, the buyer should be the key person in setting the tone, in establishing priorities, and in interacting. The buyer is the individual responsible for selecting a supplier and negotiating prices. Without buyer involvement, prompt corrective action may not occur and confusion may result—especially when a supplier is being considered for further purchase. The buyer also provides the channel for monetary charges to the supplier.

TELEPHONE CONTACT

The telephone is a fast and effective method of communication with the supplier about nonconforming goods and problems. Since the parts are not directly available to the supplier, however, a telephone discussion can lead to misunderstandings. Due to other pressures on the supplier, a phone call may fail to produce effective corrective action. A follow-up call is usually needed in order to confirm the need for corrective action or to assure that action was taken. In all cases, it is important that the call be made in a professional manner, and that all information affecting the discrepancy be available at that time. This will reduce confusion and make the call more effective. If too many problems are occurring to allow calling all the vendors involved, a few problem vendors can usually be identified for initial action. Multiple defects from the same vendors provide likely candidates for most effective use of time.

As part of an effective quality system, there should be a log of the phone call—containing the name of the individual called, date, main elements discussed, and date of promised action.

WRITTEN NOTIFICATION

Although phone contact has its advantages, it doesn't provide a written response by the vendor. An effective and inexpensive system for notifying vendors of defects can be developed through the use of a multiple copy form. The form, consisting of four copies, provides: (1) a permanent record of the defect and disposition of material, (2) a copy to transmit to the vendor for analysis and corrective action (copy 2), (3) a copy for company quality control organization (copy 3; this copy can also be used in a follow-up file to provide a reminder that a written vendor response is needed), and (4) a copy for return with the defective material to supplier if the material is being returned.

Timely transmittal of the form is important. A good system insures that the request for corrective action is transmitted to the supplier within twenty-four hours of discovery of the defect. Timeliness of the transmittal can prevent the supplier from shipping further goods with the same problem, resulting in another rejection. Many vendors will call back upon receipt of the malfunctioning goods, to obtain more details or seek information that will clarify a discrepancy.

As with the phone call, care must be taken in describing a defect so that as much information as possible is given. The description of the defect also must be accurate and clear. It is easy to fall into a trap of describing a defect as, "the hole size is too large," or "the resistance is too high." Even if there were only one hole in the part, or one resistance measurement, these are not adequate descriptions. The defect description should include the following as a minimum:

- The characteristic that is nonconforming
- The test or inspection equipment used to evaluate the part
- Significant environmental conditions present during the discovery of the defect
- The frequency with which the defect has occurred

The following description is more appropriate than "the hole is too large" and is more likely to result in corrective action by a supplier.

> *The 1.000 ± .002 located as shown on Sheet 2 grid A-1 of print 329Y634 measures oversized 1.0025 to 1.003. The hole was measured by using wedged plug gauges. Twelve of 125 pieces measured exceed print requirements. Similar defects were found on 2 of the last 3 lots received.*

Leaving out any portion of this information will tend to delay obtaining effective corrective action.

INTERNAL ACTIONS

Communicating with the supplier doesn't complete the total cycle. Internal actions at the user's facility may be required to reeducate inspectors, revise inspection planning to assure finding the defect on future lots, or revise blueprints to provide clarification. Whatever is done, however, should be communicated to the supplier to assure adequate supplier effort in resolving future problems.

STEPS IN CORRECTIVE ACTION

Corrective action involves two processes:

1. Solving particular problems
2. Identifying significant problems from available records of failures and discrepancies

The steps in a valid corrective action system might be defined as follows:

1. Problem recognition and identification
2. Gathering of information from appropriate sources
3. Evaluation
4. Generation of alternative solutions
5. Selection of a solution from alternatives
6. Follow-up to secure action
7. Secure awareness of the problem on the part of all concerned, including management
8. Record and disseminate information and evaluate results of action taken so that problems are resolved and do not recur

VISIT TO THE SUPPLIER FACILITY

Visiting the vendor as part of discrepancy analysis and corrective action implementation should not be overlooked. There are many advantages to visiting the supplier, but there are certain limitations also. Besides providing an opportunity for assessing or reassessing the supplier's quality and manufacturing system, it provides firsthand observation of the supplier's attitude and approach to quality, technical strengths, handling of defectives, and management commitment to resolution of quality problems. To illustrate, take a case in which a common part discrepancy might be revealed by a mechanical measurement made using a surface plate. Finding the supplier's surface plate covered with dust provides information on the supplier's commitment to meeting print requirements and following the basics of an inspection system. One other advantage of visiting the supplier is the possibility of encountering additional problems, which, if not caught in the early stages, would become more serious and result in subsequent rejections.

Key management individuals can also be contacted to assure proper priorities and to obtain a commitment to resolve discrepancies and perform the required corrective action.

QUALITY AUDITS

Audits for quality can be of several types:

1. *System Audits*—to determine the effectiveness of the overall quality system and the degree to which quality objectives are achieved
2. *Product Audits*—to determine fitness for use of the product by the intended customer
3. *Procedure Audits*—to ascertain whether established procedures are being followed by inspectors, testers, operators, material handlers, etc.

The quality audit provides a further opportunity to see exactly how the supplier assures quality. What measures are used and

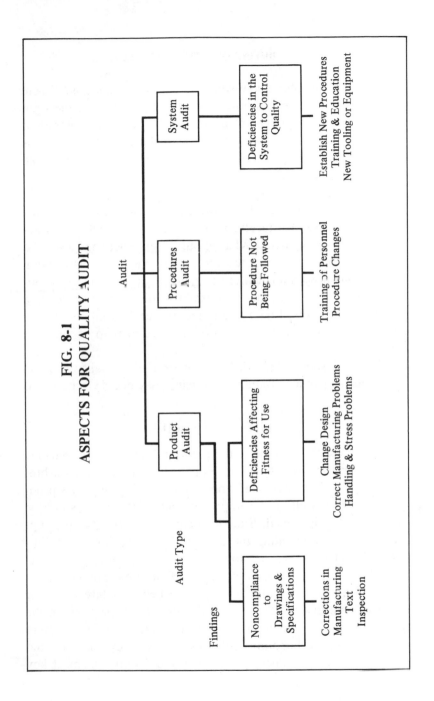

FIG. 8-1
ASPECTS FOR QUALITY AUDIT

how does the supplier know what the outgoing quality is? Where are the checks made and how involved is each? Were the right people at the supplier plant aware of the rejected material or complaints from customers? If not, are there really provisions for communicating problems to the people who can really take the corrective action?

This is an opportunity to see how rejections are actually handled by the supplier. It is also a chance to examine records of past discrepancies received from users to see what was actually done about them. What about cases where the user did not return nonconforming items to the supplier? Was any action actually taken by the supplier? In general, it is a chance to observe what actions are taken to establish disposition, corrective action, verification of the fix, and recurrence prevention—the final determination of whether corrective action is to be successful.

Figure 8 shows three different aspects of a quality audit of a supplier—or of a self-audit a company may decide to perform.

VISIT BY SUPPLIER

Inviting a vendor to come to the plant and review a discrepancy provides an opportunity to develop a meaningful relationship. During the visit, a review of where and how the supplier's product is used as well as the impact of part discrepancies can be discussed and displayed. Situations can be presented to the supplier, such as illustrating the difficulty of repairing items, impact of defect upon employee productivity and production schedule, and effect on the customer if the final product is defective. The visit can give a supplier a better picture of his or her responsibility and the role of the supplier's materials in the finished product. The supplier could also assist in development of procedures for handling problems, discrepancy analysis, and design review. The visit also enables the supplier to meet key individuals who are involved in supplier product design, production, and quality control.

RETURNING THE LOT

Returning the rejected lot or material is an effective method of demonstrating the desire to obtain corrective action. It provides the vendor firsthand information and an opportunity to analyze the defect. It also places the responsibility for sorting and/or rework at the origin of the discrepancy. Financial burdens are charged to the vendor in the form of transportation fees, lost productivity, and delayed billing. It is advisable to include a clear description of the nonconformity with the material and to have the defective parts clearly segregated from the remainder of the lot. Any further information useful to the supplier in correcting or sorting the defects is important.

CHARGING SUPPLIER
FOR DEFECTS

All user systems should have a means for requesting monetary payment from suppliers when the buyer's operation does sorting, retesting, or rework caused by a supplier's nonconforming goods. These should be developed to include the purchasing operation and coordination through the buyer. The matter of whether the supplier will pay the full requested amount becomes negotiable. The supplier may refuse payment or may pay only a fraction of costs incurred. Even though no payment is received, a record of the cost incurred as a result of a supplier nonconformity provides the information for the buyer that will assist in negotiating new purchases.

If the requested charges are reasonable and reflect only the supplier's liability because of the discrepancies, there should be a good chance of collection from the supplier.

CONSEQUENTIAL AND
INCIDENTAL DAMAGES

We can define "consequential damages" as those resulting from nonconformity of an item, such as user repair costs, downtime, injuries, etc. These can often be substantial, amounting to more than the costs of the supplier items themselves. Suppliers are aware of this, so they frequently try to disclaim any responsibilities beyond the value of the item supplied. The Uniform Commercial Code (UCC) recognizes the user's right to consequential damages, but points out that the user has certain responsibilities in identifying and preventing use of nonconforming items.

The UCC is clearer in stating supplier responsibility for "incidental damages," which are expenses reasonably incurred by the user in inspecting, receipt, handling, care, and custody of nonconforming goods. The user, however, must demonstrate that the method of computing these charges is reasonable. Further, a user is expected to have reasonable inspection procedures upon receipt of goods. The cost of a buyer's efforts to get a purchased item to work properly, however, can be deemed proper charges to the supplier.

MATERIAL REVIEW BOARD

Some facilities utilize the Material Review Board (MRB) concept to assure adequate corrective action. The MRB would consist of an engineer and a quality control representative, at minimum. The board would meet periodically to review defective material, determine the cause, define the corrective action to be taken, and decide upon disposition of the defective material (such as repair, using it in the existing state, or scrap). Records of MRB actions are maintained, and recurrences of similar defects at a later time indicate inadequate corrective action.

PROBLEM VENDORS

How can we determine which suppliers should appear on the list of problem vendors? Problems holding up shipments, production lines, or use of equipment in the field almost automatically cause the responsible vendor to be placed on the list. A policy could be established by which a vendor's name is added, for example, whenever 4 percent of the vendor's lots have been rejected over the past three months. This criteria could be tightened or relaxed as needed. The degree of seriousness of the defects causing the rejection should be considered also, since parts used "as is" create less trouble than those sent back, repaired, or scrapped.

In some cases the solution may be as simple as changing a part number; in other cases a process or design at the vendor's plant may need to be changed. Sometimes the contractor may need to send technical assistance to help at the supplier's plant. This assistance would not, however, remove the responsibility for solving problems from the supplier.

RECURRENCE
OF DEFECTIVES

Sometimes a company's quality objectives may allow a certain percentage of defectives on the premise that zero defects is not economically practical. In that case it becomes necessary to be able to determine when recurrences of a defect exceed the allowable percentage. This makes it necessary to record defects, evaluate the quality data, and identify significant problems. When the recurrence of a defect is considered significant, it is necessary to take corrective action. A machine that is not set properly may produce 5 percent defects instead of ½ percent, as allowed. It may not be easy to notice this excessive level without recording and evaluating data.

ATTACKING THE
QUALITY PROBLEMS

At some point a company may recognize that quality problems exist with vendors. However, it may be too late to implement all of the techniques that constitute a good quality control program. Subcontracts may already exist without adequate standards. Or, we may have a good program, but there are still quality problems. How do we get started in doing something to improve the situation? First, purchasing must take the lead. The purchasing manager must make his or her personnel aware of their responsibilities. One way to start is to identify the biggest problems. They might be the most pressing problems, or the vendors with an accumulation of lesser problems, or a combination of both. Most important, however, this gives us something to start working on. Second, the purchasing agent can contact each problem vendor and let the vendor know of his or her status as a problem vendor. The purchasing agent may worry that vendor X is the only available supplier, or the supplier may be offended and drop the buying company because, from the vendor's point of view, the company is only a small customer. That attitude, however, is not acceptable, and when pressure is applied, alternate sources can usually be found.

The problem vendors should be brought into the plant. It is usually most effective to have supplier management people come in and see the problems that their defectives are causing. This works better than sending contractor personnel to see and hear the supplier's pitch on how good they are and see how nice their plant looks. In other words, when the supplier comes in, the company controls the topics of discussion and who participates. It is pointed out that the supplier has a problem that must be solved in order to meet the subcontract requirements, and it is the supplier's responsibility to solve it. Acceptance of responsibility by the supplier goes a long way toward arriving at a successful resolution of the problem.

WEAKNESSES AND STRENGTHS OF A CORRECTIVE ACTION SYSTEM

We have said that successful corrective action means permanent correction of a problem. There are, however, several weaknesses in corrective action systems that are important to identify:

1. Emphasis on quick fixes to make the product usable
2. Excessive delays in communicating information on failures to those responsible
3. Jumping at conclusions as to causes of nonconformitics
4. Failure to bring problems to the attention of top management
5. Neglect of deficiencies that come to the supplier's attention after shipment

A well-defined corrective action system will contain the following elements:

1. Discrepancies are well-defined and reported quickly.
2. Each problem is validated to establish its importance with respect to effect on quality of the final product, costs, and impact on schedules.
3. A diagnosis is made of causes of the nonconformity and the corrective action needed to permanently resolve the problem.
4. Assignment of responsibility for corrective action is made and a schedule established for completion.
5. Determination is made as to whether other suppliers' items have similar problems.
6. Follow up is done to ascertain that the problem has been solved.

STRATEGY AND
MOTIVATION FOR
SUPPLIER QUALITY

In dealing with strategy, it is necessary to relate differing interpretations of the term "quality." Earlier we dealt with quality as conformance to specifications and fitness for use. This objective quality is a measurable factor. Marketing texts, however, in using the term, would say that the Cadillac is a higher-quality automobile than the Chevrolet. The intended meaning is that the Cadillac has greater performance expectations, or in other words, is more luxurious. Another meaning of quality is more subjective, involving quality as perceived by the customer, whose failure to perceive the desired quality results in reduced sales of the product. A firm, in defining its strategy, must deal with each of the concepts separately—and together as a composite strategy.

The strive for productivity is also a key part of strategy. In past years quality was often viewed in opposition to productivity; that is, increasing quality reduced productivity. The key, however, is the point at which productivity is measured. The traditional practice was to measure productivity at the end of the production line. A more realistic procedure measures productivity so as to include customer acceptance of products; products returned by the customer are subtracted from productivity figures. As a result, acceptable quality becomes a key factor in increasing productivity. Dr. A. V. Fiegenbaum[1], widely recognized quality control authority, speaks of the "hidden factory capacity" required to do repair and rework, in some cases up to 30 percent of the normal plant capacity. If rework and repair were eliminated, the additional capacity (space and employees) would be available to perform productive work.

PURCHASING STRATEGY

Purchasing strategy is part of company strategy. In carrying out company strategy, it is necessary for purchasing managers to:

- Understand the purchasing environment
- Anticipate and monitor changes in the environment
- Work closely with suppliers or potential suppliers, facilitating the exchange of information
- Work closely with other functional areas within the firm
- Identify threats and opportunities related to purchasing objectives
- Identify the firm's strengths and weaknesses in light of the current environment
- Define strategic alternatives
- Select courses of action applicable to the company and its products

Concurrent with the above steps, it is necessary to:

- Identify critical materials based on threats to supply
- Identify critical purchases based on difficult requirements
- Consider long-term and short-term needs

1. A. V. Fiegenbaum, *Total Quality Control*. McGraw-Hill Book Company, New York, 1983, p. 46.

ALTERNATIVES WHERE
THREATS OF DEFICIENCIES
ARE IDENTIFIED

In the strategic planning process, the firm may identify situations in which available suppliers are not able to meet projected requirements. The projected deficiencies may occur in capacity, cost, or quality. Where these threats to future requirements are identified, the firm has certain options:

1. Look for new sources
2. Provide selected suppliers with financial or technological assistance
3. Develop internal capability
4. Motivate suppliers to develop their own additional capability

During the early 1980s, progressive U.S. firms have tended to implement a combination of options 2 and 4 as a partnership-like strategy of working closely with certain suppliers to furnish long-term needs.

Following the lead of the Japanese, some firms have sought ways of improving quality of supplier products and lowering costs. The trend has been to place reliance on suppliers that historically have provided quality products, rather than on sampling techniques designed to determine quality for acceptance or rejection of individual deliveries. One way of accomplishing this has been to change the strategy of dealing with suppliers from one of hostility to one of working together more closely. This has resulted in supplier strategies that do the following:

1. Involve suppliers early in the development of new products
2. Give suppliers improved forecasts of both short-term and long-term needs

3. Decrease the number of suppliers for each part or material to a few sources that consistently have shown the ability to furnish quality
4. Decrease the number of suppliers further by procuring several items from one source (The total reduction in number of suppliers from [3] and [4] combined may be as high as a factor of ten to one.)
5. Work more closely with each supplier to achieve certification and assure the ability to furnish quality products consistently
6. Reduce inventories of purchased goods
7. Eliminate or reduce the necessity for inspection of goods upon receipt
8. Enter into long-term subcontracts (three to five years or more)
9. Help suppliers implement statistical and/or computerized process controls

The reduction in number of suppliers, and the long-term commitments, permit suppliers to install more efficient manufacturing and inspection equipment and to invest in skilled personnel. Both of these factors result in long-term cost reductions and quality improvements, to the benefit of both the selling and buying organization.

These strategies have resulted in cost savings in the following ways:

1. Fewer lots are rejected and returned to the supplier.
2. Inspection upon receipt at buyer's facility can be eliminated.
3. Rework or repair related to use of defectives in assembly can be reduced.
4. Inventory costs are reduced as lots are delivered as needed for manufacturing.

LONGER-TERM RELATIONSHIPS

The well-known management consultant Peter F. Drucker stated that we could learn only two things from Japanese management: (1) an effective program cannot be built on adversarial relations, and (2) responsible employees can be created by giving them responsibilities. These same concepts can be applied to suppliers. First, collaboration with suppliers, rather than an adversary relationship, can lead to effective programs; and second, responsible suppliers can result from delegation of more responsibility to them.

Both buyers and suppliers need the stability and security provided by establishing longer-term relationships. These long-term relationships must be built up through efforts of both purchaser and suppliers. Each must make concessions to the other in order to arrive at a relationship satisfactory to both. Continuing coordination and cooperation are important in retaining the relationship, once it is established.

Why have firms—which for so long strongly emphasized price competition—changed direction to place greater emphasis on the long-term relationship?

1. They have found that this results in fewer quality problems and fewer missed delivery dates.
2. When there is a supply/shortage problem, the firms with the long-term relationship suffer less than the opportunistic buyers.
3. Product quality is better when the supplier senses the potential loss of a relationship developed over time.
4. Frequent changes in suppliers require renewed periods of learning to work together.
5. Product innovations result in design changes. Implementation of changes in requirements is less costly and time consuming when a long-term relationship has been developed.

6. If either party runs into a financial crisis, concessions are more likely if a long-term relationship exists.
7. Cooperation helps minimize inventory carrying costs.
8. Last, but not least, the firm and its suppliers can work together to solve technical problems to achieve quality improvement in the products.

There are precautions, however, that must be taken to avoid a drift into a complacent atmosphere. A buyer can reinforce this strategy by using certain tactics over the life of the relationship:

1. Supplier audit
2. Records of supplier quality
3. A continuing program involving checking with other potential suppliers for cost quotations
4. Changing suppliers or going to second sources when the evidence so indicates

Some other cases can be cited that duplicate the Japanese experiences. Some U.S. companies ran into difficulties in the 1970s when collaborative relationships with suppliers were abandoned (*Business Week* [Feb. 16, 1981]: 53).

Stronger commitments to suppliers over the long term do not diminish the importance of certain other factors. The doors should be left open for new suppliers when new technologies are applicable to company products. Suppliers in turn are expected to contribute cost-cutting ideas and they are expected to understand the goals, products, and needs of the company.

JUST-IN-TIME

Many companies are merging the "just-in-time" concept with the long-term relationship in formulating procurement strategy. This concept achieves the objectives of low (or no) inventory along with few (or no) defects in supplied goods. Under the just-in-time concept as used widely in Japan, goods in relatively small quantities (such as a week's supply) are sent directly to the production line with little or no incoming inspection. A prerequisite is the certified supplier—usually under a long-term working agreement—who can be depended upon to control quality and furnish defect-free goods.

There are several other considerations, however, that are important in the implementation of this dual strategy of just-in-time and long-term certified suppliers, as follows:

1. *Geographic proximity.* It is much easier to control transit times if the suppliers' plants are close to the using facility. This is common in Japan, where Toyota, for example, has most of its suppliers within sixty miles of the assembly plant.
2. *Reliable transportation.* This may involve some company-owned vehicles in case of labor stoppages.
3. *Efficient logistics.* The ability to deliver goods to the point of usage efficiently and without damage is essential.
4. *Reduced number of suppliers.* Because of the investment needed in time and dollars, a reduction in the total number of suppliers becomes a necessity.
5. *Broader knowledge by purchasing personnel,* especially in the area of quality control.
6. *Centralization of purchasing.* In some cases, multidivision firms have assigned to a single plant the overall responsibility for purchase of particular parts used throughout the corporation. This responsibility could include requirements definition, procurement, and quality assurance.

CERTIFICATION OF SUPPLIERS

Several firms have integrated a "supplier product certification program" into their strategy. This program consists of:

1. A thorough review of suppliers' quality control capabilities
2. Evaluating supplier capability based on projected order sizes
3. Working with suppliers to help them develop capabilities
4. Communicating the importance of quality goals
5. Obtaining acceptance of quality requirements through participation by the suppliers in establishing the requirements
6. Identifying critical components of supplied products
7. Performing an analysis of what might go wrong with products, and what the effect would be
8. Assuring feedback of quality information to supplier from buyer

Those suppliers who meet exacting standards are certified for specific parts. This program is then a prerequisite to just-in-time supply programs.

AUTOMATION

Computer-based measuring devices have been developed in recent years. Their use permits (1) measurement of parts rapidly and with a high degree of accuracy, (2) integration of the measurement into the manufacturing process, and (3) charting the measurements to determine process patterns. This allows the manufacturer to move in the direction of totally eliminating production of defective items.

DRAWBACKS

Companies planning to change their procurement stragegy to incorporate these ideas should not expect immediate results. Japanese firms and U.S. firms that have achieved results with these strategies have spent several years accomplishing them. It will involve an investment in time and money, with returns not immediately evident.

ELEMENTS OF STRATEGY

In formulating supplier-quality tactics and strategy, it is interesting to examine how they fit into overall strategy formulation. In the diagnosis of any strategic problem we can divide the elements into *controllable actions*—those under company control—and *uncontrollable events*—those not under company control, such as competitor's actions, consumer thinking, and government policies. It would be a mistake for a company to assume that supplier actions are not under buyer control, since prior chapters have defined the many ways in which a company can control the quality of purchased goods. Extensive inspection of incoming goods is actually a strategy based upon inability to control quality of supplied goods.

Another important aspect of strategy formulation is to ascertain the significance of alternative outcomes. In the case of supplier quality, we have discussed its substantial impact upon in-plant productivity and also the impact upon future business of the company based upon the product quality perceived by the customer.

END OBJECTIVES

The final judge of success of a strategy for quality is in the marketplace. The customer will respond by purchasing those products with greatest perceived value. In cases where the use life of the product is short—such as food, household supplies, or other frequently purchased items—the perceived quality can be based on fitness for use perceived from prior purchases of the product. In longer-life items such as home appliances or automobiles, the perceived value is based more on other factors. These factors relate back to the quality strategy in that a firm must determine customer satisfiers, and how customers distinguish good products from those perceived as poorer.

IMPLEMENTING STRATEGIES

Establishing a strategy based on this concern can take many forms. The strategy might be included in other overall business objectives. For instance, the Motorola Company set a corporate goal to improve total quality by a factor of ten. Recognizing the contributions supplies make to product quality, the Motorola Company has established a strategy that encourages suppliers to improve their performance. As another example, the Texas Instruments Corporation has developed a supplier strategy and has established a goal, in order to maintain supplier quality performance, of meeting or exceeding a 98 percent lot acceptance rate. Besides measuring the supplier's performance, Texas Instruments also measures the supplier's schedule performance by recording the number of lots received early, on time, and late. Delivery performance is measured in terms of days before or after scheduled delivery. The Texas Instruments supplier program includes elements that might easily be a part of anyone's program, such as:

- Vendor Conferences
- Material/Quality teams
- Audits
- Negotiating teams
- Quarterly management reviews
- Option/Corporate agreements

In its vendor program, Texas Instruments has documented its strategy and developed activities associated with the strategy. The activities include vendor conferences, in which the vendor is appraised of the program through a formal presentation.

QUALITY COSTS

The cost of quality is often limited by some firms to the costs of inspection and test. In the past, this has often led to strategies that result in noncompetitive products. Any successful quality strategy must consider the cost of nonconformance as compared to the cost of conformance. Payments for rework, calling products back from the user, and other costs of nonconformance are all factors to be recognized.

Each functional department in an organization must be able to justify itself by measuring its costs and comparing the costs to the department's contributions to company objectives and profits. Quality control is not excepted. Thus, it becomes important to determine an overall cost of quality control. This can best be accomplished by segregating quality costs into four categories.

1. *Prevention*—Prevention costs are those costs associated with planning and carrying out the quality program tasks that take place before the product is manufactured. The following are examples of tasks that can be classified as defect prevention:
   a. Design review
   b. Employee training and certification programs
   c. Supplier evaluation before awarding subcontracts
   d. Quality control engineering, including design of special tooling and equipment
   e. Process controls to assure that manufacturing processes hold product tolerances

2. *Evaluation Costs*—Evaluation (or appraisal) costs are those costs associated with measuring conformance of products to standards, including inspection and tests. The following are examples of tasks for which the costs fall into this category:
   a. Inspection and testing of incoming parts and materials from suppliers

b. Inspection and testing of materials, parts, subassemblies, or completed products manufactured in the plant

c. Cost of products destroyed or damaged by destructive or life tests

d. Calibration and maintenance of inspection gauges and test equipment

e. Quality data collection, records, and reports

3. *Internal Failure*—Internal failures are those that occur prior to shipment (or while the producing company still owns the product). These costs result from defective products (products failing to meet requirements). The cost of the following fall into this category:

a. Value of products scrapped

b. Rework costs to make defective items conform to standards

c. Cost associated with analysis of failures or defects to determine cause

d. Cost of reinspection or retest of products that have been reworked

e. Reduced value of products sold as seconds due to defects

4. *External Failure*—Failures that take place after the customer assumes ownership of a product contribute to this category of costs. These costs include the following through the period of warranty:

a. Replacement of defectives

b. Repair costs

c. Costs of receiving and processing complaints

d. Liability of producer due to product hazards, usually incurred through liability insurance costs or litigation

e. Loss of future orders or damage to reputation due to defectives received by customers

QUALITY COST TRADE-OFFS

The cost of quality can be portrayed as a trade-off as illustrated by figure 9. The direct costs include prevention and evaluation. As these are reduced, the number of defectives increases. As the defect level increases, the failure costs increase.

The total costs are the sum of direct costs and failure costs. At the minimum of the total cost curve, the optimum mixture of effort is indicated. More and more firms are deciding that their optimum cost point is at a very low level of defectives, possibly close to zero. This follows from several factors:

1. The high cost of lost sales due to perceived low quality by customers
2. High labor costs related to return/repair of failed products after shipment to customer
3. Feasibility of in-process controls based on automated equipment and statistical controls, jointly resulting in close to zero defectives

SUPPLIER QUALITY VS. COSTS

The vendor quality strategy must be based on cost versus quality and the impact on the firm's business. Determining this cost traceable to the vendor quality program and quality deficiencies is not always easy. The elements could include:

- Total value of material received compared with total inventory
- Cost of extra inventory due to anticipated problems
- Cost of extra inventory due to nonconforming material held for disposition
- Cost of rework due to supplier defective material
- Cost of scrap due to supplier nonconforming material

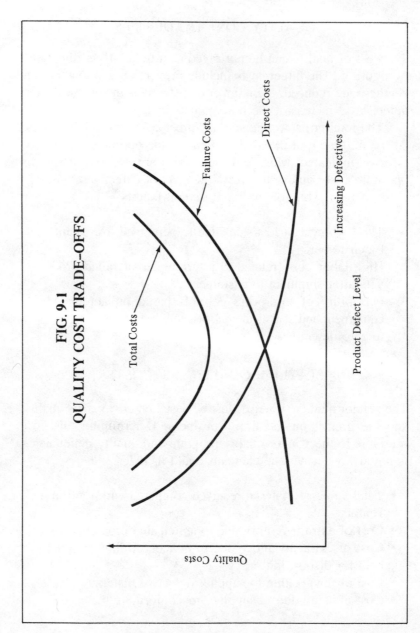

FIG. 9-1
QUALITY COST TRADE-OFFS

- Cost of production delays and lack of work, due to defective vendor material
- Cost to inspect material
- Cost to evaluate new suppliers
- Cost to perform supplier surveys
- Cost to visit supplier to solve problems
- Amount collected from suppliers resulting from defect claims
- Cost of lost business due to supplier quality deficiencies
- Cost to evaluate supplier defects
- Cost of inspection equipment
- Cost of holding material awaiting inspection
- Cost to maintain and analyze records on supplier performance
- Cost to handle defective supplier material

VENDOR COSTS

Unless vendor costs are properly assessed, the full impact of supplier material on the user's facility cannot be determined. The measure of this impact can be achieved by determining the value of total cost of goods sold as compared to the value of vendor material received. The higher this ratio, the greater the supplier's impact on the user's business. While the source of these costs was defined earlier, some further aspects should be considered.

Incoming evaluation has become increasingly costly and often exceedingly difficult. Complex material and parts result in high expenditures for test equipment to evaluate complex systems. For some electronic components, equipment to perform evaluative tests at receiving inspection can cost hundreds of thousands of dollars. Equipment for measuring mechanical characteristics of piece parts in general is also very expensive, difficult to obtain, and not thorough in assuring that all dimensional characteristics meet requirements.

In assessing the need for inspection manpower, the user should recognize how the level of inspection is related to the number of parts received versus the number of lots received. If sampling inspection is used, inspection cost is related to the number of lots. In fact, during periods of low business the level of incoming inspection manpower requirements may not reduce significantly since only lot sizes might be reduced. If the number of lots is also reduced, incoming inspection manpower revisions can be considered. In the case where 100 percent inspection is performed, the cost of inspection manpower is directly related to production needs and the amount of material being received.

In any case, many users are choosing to establish programs that coordinate the supplier documentation as well as test verification data to demonstrate that each unit meets contract requirements and performance specifications. These high costs also explain why managers are moving toward programs which emphasize placing more responsibility upon the supplier to provide 100 percent acceptable products. Good quality products received by the user's facility can be placed directly into stock or can be placed directly at the production line for immediate use.

If confidence in a supplier is not achieved, the user's overall inventories increase due to delays at receiving inspection. The concept of just-in-time reduces these inventory costs since vendor goods can be placed immediately at the production site. It is advantageous for the user to be able to depend on the supplier's quality system since in-process checks can be performed by the supplier but are not available to the user. If this objective can be achieved, it will result in reduced expenditures by the user for equipment necessary to assess product conformance.

PROGRAM ASSESSMENT

When establishing supplier costs, the user must determine what factors it will use to evaluate the effectiveness of the quality program. Once established, the factors that are used should be budgeted and monitored to assure that conditions do not get out of control. Increases of inspection costs per lot received or per piece received can be indications of poor quality performance by the supplier. Levels of charges for scrap and rework are an indication of supplier problems also. The gathering and display of this information can be used as evidence to encourage improved vendor quality. Regardless of the action taken, without the data being displayed and presented to management, a vendor quality program will have little positive direction or aim. Management—and the supplier—will pay more attention when all the costs related to nonconformance are brought into focus.

ALTERNATIVES AVAILABLE
TO MOTIVATE SUPPLIERS

Vendor motivation can be achieved through both active and reactive means. The active motivation includes *monetary* recognition through exclusive contract awards, premium payments for product quality, or special inventory carrying payments. *Nonmonetary* recognition includes vendor awards or letters to management. The reactive means that may be classified as *monetary* include product returns, cancellation of contracts, collection of rework and scrap charges, or legal action. *Nonmonetary* reactive means include letters to management, on-site reviews, discrediting of quality image through press releases, and ALERTS or disapproved product lists.

EXCLUSIVE CONTRACT AWARD

Releasing exclusive contract awards to vendors meeting specific quality and delivery objectives is one of the methods of rewarding a supplier. It represents an important motivator. For the user, it reflects confidence and trust in the ability and capability of a supplier to furnish consistently high-quality products on schedule. For the vendor, besides the assurance of continuing business associated with good performance, it provides prestige and leads to additional business. The exclusive award can include provisions for incentive payments for both quality and delivery performance. It provides the purchaser opportunities to make a long-term contract and potentially preclude impacts of inflation by making advance purchases of material. If the supplier continues to demonstrate delivery and quality performance, the buyer's problems are reduced.

PREMIUM PAYMENTS

Premium payments provide monetary recognition for performance. The reward should be commensurate with the effort required to meet pre-established goals. If the goals are either too easily obtained or impossible to achieve, program effectiveness is undermined. Both the buyer and supplier must agree to the criteria for determining premium payment. The expectations, both in delivery and quality performance, must be measurable and pre-established. Then they must be measured on a timely basis and reported so each side can understand the progress.

Premium payments could include payment for overtime, the cost of special equipment, prepayment for long lead material, bonuses based on delivery and quality performance, and pre-planned purchase of overages. If it is successful, both the buyer and seller have much to gain from this type of program. There are dangers, however, in this approach. Why pay extra to a supplier for providing just what the contract requires anyway? A company using a premium payment plan will need to consider attitudes that may develop if the plan is used.

TOP VENDOR AWARDS

Top vendor awards, although not monetary, are important to both supplier and user. They are a demonstration to other vendors, and also a reflection of the buyer's and seller's quality. For both buyer and supplier, the awards provide a level of prestige and community recognition and an intangible measure of performance. When presented, the award should involve ceremony consistent with the award's significance. If it is a major national award, a press release should appear in an appropriate national newspaper. Releases in local newspapers are also important recognition of the performance. The ceremony should include top-level management from both the buyer's and supplier's facilities, and most importantly, participation by members of the work force.

LETTERS TO MANAGEMENT

Although not as prestigious as top vendor awards, letters to management have important roles in achieving recognition for individuals or organizations in achieving goals or putting forth special effort. Those receiving the recognition should be deserving of the letters and all individuals involved should be identified.

RETURN OF GOODS

Unless a buyer returns defective material to the supplier, the buyer may be establishing a level of acceptable quality. In other words, if a user continually accepts lots of materials that have defects or that include defective items, the supplier has little initiative to correct a problem. In fact, the supplier is led to believe that the quality provided is totally acceptable for use. If the supplier receives no communication from the user about defects, there is an implied revision to the specification concerning the quality as well as the design requirements for the product.

Product returns have several effects on the supplier. First, they result in a debit of sales to be issued to the supplier and become noticeable as extra expense due to the shipping costs incurred. In some cases, shipping and handling costs are more expensive than the material returned. Product return provides the opportunity for the supplier to have firsthand evidence of the quality required by the user as well as firsthand evidence of the defective material. Product returns also result in lost productivity due to the fact that they require rework in the factory and additional handling and cost. The product return may also assure management attention at the user's facility since the return could result in low levels of productivity. It is important for the user to audit product return and product acceptance practices to assure that implied specification revisions are not occurring through continued use of defective material through Material Review Board actions.

CANCELLATION OF CONTRACTS

Cancellation of a contract due to poor quality or performance is a reaction to continuing problems with a supplier and a perception that the supplier is unable to correct situations that are encountered. Cancellation of the contract, if based on poor quality performance, may have a heavy monetary impact on the supplier, since material may have been purchased for use in fulfilling the contract, and work may be in process. These parts may not be usable for any other contract the supplier has. In addition, the cancellation creates a problem of work force instability for the supplier, especially if the contract represented a sizable portion of the business.

This action usually reflects a user's attitude, which is that the supplier is unable to correct serious quality deficiencies that exist in the processing of products at the supplier's facility. Generally it is not desirable from either the user's or supplier's standpoint, since the user is faced with the responsibility of developing an alternate method of obtaining the material or process. It may mean program delays or line shutdowns at the user facility. However, an alternative supplier may be the user's only method of achieving acceptable product performance.

REWORK AND
SCRAP CHARGES

An incentive that users often do not utilize is the charging of rework and scrap to the supplier, either by direct invoicing or reduction of payments on incoming invoices. The rework and scrap charges involved at the user facilities may be a substantial portion of the original invoice amount. The fact that a charge is being made to the vendor for rework or scrap incurred by the user generally involves the buyer to the extent that the charge must be negotiated with the supplier. In addition, it brings the defect to the attention of both the buyer and supplier and emphasizes the impact of the defect on the user's system. It is another communication method that could potentially result in corrective action efforts at the supplier's facility to assure that additional charges will not be incurred for future defective material. The supplier may choose to perform the rework to minimize the charge involved. However, due to production constraints, the user may insist that rework be accomplished at the user's facility by first sorting the material and then repairing the defective material at the supplier's facility. If sorting is accomplished by the supplier at the user's facility, significant travel costs may be involved, which will affect the overall profits of the supplier.

Even if an acceptable rework or scrap charge to the supplier cannot be negotiated by the buyer, information concerning the levels of rework and scrap resulting from a defective product become an item allowing for negotiation of reduced cost on a new product or a product yet to be shipped. The amount and number of charges made for poor quality performance and resulting in rework or sorting at the user's facility become a measure for the buyer in determining whether future contracts might better be awarded to a higher-cost bidder. In this case, the lack of responsiveness by the supplier could result in loss of contracts for new business.

LEGAL ACTION

Legal action may be the most undesirable way of achieving resolution of a supplier-user problem since it is time consuming, costly, and has an indeterminate result. Neither the supplier nor user can predetermine the judgment that will be made in court. Quite often there are documentation conflicts in contracts and contract clauses resulting in legal decisions not satisfactory to either side. Legal actions are a burden to both the user and supplier because of the cost and time involved. However, they should be used if the situation calls for such action. Essentially, the contemplation of legal action is an incentive to try to resolve the problem by other means.

ON-SITE REPRESENTATIVE

The control of a product by a user through the use of a representative at the supplier facility could result in some loss of manufacturing control by the supplier. The supplier's flexibility in production as well as manpower usage become constrained by the presence of an on-site representative. On-site representatives generally require additional technical support not planned for by the supplier. Their presence can be positive, however, if the representatives are used to establish better communication channels between the supplier and the user and to reduce difficulties as they arise. The on-site individual can be used to interpret specifications as well as to expedite interpretations of contract requirements through contacting of user individuals not generally available to the supplier.

Other types of on-site reviews could include a visit by several user representatives—including the buyer, quality control, manufacturing, or other technical individuals. This review team could become the impetus for a stringent audit of supplier facilities and processes to determine quality approach as well as conformance to requirements. An interruption of the daily flow of products, as well as of production, could result—especially if supplier-user communications are strained. In the right atmosphere, visits can be positive in that user problems and lack of correlation of techniques could be uncovered and resolved at the time of the visit, and supplier systems proven to be acceptable from a product and quality standpoint. In general, however, the underlying threat of on-site visits is a motivation to the supplier to seek solutions to problems beforehand.

PRESS RELEASES AND ALERTS

The supplier's quality image can be discredited by the user through press releases documenting receipt of poor quality products from the supplier. Documentation of poor quality can also be made in GIDEP ALERTS, which provide information to governmental as well as industry users of products that material is defective in a particular way.

Both the press release and ALERTS can result in significant loss of business due to the discrediting of the product's quality image. Both receive wide distribution to existing users as well as potential users of products in flow. The ALERT to governmental individuals often becomes a demand to evaluate product conformance from the supplier of any material in stock at their facility. It also demands review of product applications to determine whether material placed in assembly is to be removed due to the product deficiencies. These types of activities become the focus for loss of business, product returns, and stringent audits of production facilities by both commercial and military organizations.

A typical example of this situation was provided when recent press releases documented the nonconformance of suppliers in conducting reliability tests on products shipped. The press releases indicated that while the suppliers documented conformance to requirements for reliability tests, the tests were not actually being performed. As a result of failure to perform the reliability testing, defective products were shipped to various user facilities. It is obvious that press releases concerning both the poor performance of American automotive products in comparison to Japanese automotive products seriously affected the American market for many years, until the American automotive industry was able to demonstrate its ability to compete with the Japanese from a quality standpoint. The loss of national revenue, as well as the loss of jobs, was significant, to say the least.

MOTIVATION AND LONG-TERM RELATIONSHIPS

In the relationship between a firm and its suppliers, there are two ways in which motivation for quality can be obtained under the teamwork concept:

1. The continuance of the long-term relationship in itself furnishes a motivation for the supplier to provide quality in the products or services.
2. The experienced firm can assist the supplier in the implementation of concepts that have proved successful in improving quality and productivity. The firm can supply film presentations to the supplier, which can be shown to personnel at all working levels. These presentations would show how the products are used and the importance of furnishing products without defects, which will perform properly when placed in use.

The theory *Z* concept of management also fits well with the motivation for quality and strategy for long-term relationships with suppliers. Dr. William G. Ouchi defines a way of managing people that focuses on a strong company commitment, a policy of retaining long-term employees, very careful evaluation of employees prior to promotion, development of managers to operate in several functional areas, consensus decision making, and close communications.[2]

Quality problems often result from the inability of someone at the supplier's facility to obtain an answer to a question, such as a question about interpretation of a requirement. Some firms have hot lines through which anyone at the supplier facility can call and ask a question. The inability to obtain an answer to a question is a great demotivator. Also, a response to a question often results in clarification or even a requirement change.

The objective of a motivation program is to arrive at a position where supplier personnel accept responsibility for quality. This depends on letting the supplier have some latitude in deciding how requirements are to be achieved. The primary motivation to the supplier is the expectation of continuing business over an extended period of time as long as quality products are supplied, on schedule, and at a competitive price.

In any quality plan, we come back to the fact that the responsibility for quality rests with the purchasing organization. Other parts of the organization have a part to play, but purchasing must take over and administer the strategy in order to achieve quality from suppliers.

2. William G Ouchi, *Theory Z: How American Business Can Meet the Japanese Challenge* (Reading: Addison-Wesley, 1981).

INDEX